Endorsements

"The power of God is the only solution in a world riddled with darkness and despair. We've tried every solution of man yet many are still lost, broken and confused. I believe as you read this book that the practicality of the power of God would become your greatest reality. May the final words of Jesus on the earth become one of the greatest chapters of your story. It's time for a church who's clothed in power to show the world the truth of who our God is."

Ross Johnston, Revivalist
California Will Be Saved

"Powerless Christianity is a tragic oxymoron. Scripture tells us that we have been given an anointing which enables our inabilities and empowers us to represent the kingdom of God on this planet. Andrew has written a timely book on a timeless subject. *Clothed With Power* doesn't just talk about power, it gives you principles and insights to make it a reality in your life!"

Sean Smith
Author of *Prophetic Evangelism* and *I Am Your Sign*
Co-host of "Keep It 100" Podcast
www.seanandchristasmith.com

"God is looking for those who are carriers of the Presence and power of God on their lives! In Andrew's new book called *Clothed With Power*, you will be activated in both the miracle power of Jesus and an intimate friendship with the Holy Spirit. Prepare to be launched into the next level of knowing God more and making him known to people around you in everyday life."

Jerame Nelson
Author of *Portals of Revelation* and
Burning Ones: Calling Forth a Generation of Dread Champions

"What can I say? I love this book *Clothed with Power* for three reasons (I can give more!). It is essential, practical, and anointed. Let me expound. It is essential. It highlights what the church should be, as defined by Jesus. We cannot be otherwise. The body of Christ has to learn and re-learn these truths if it is to re-present Christ effectively to the world. It is practical. I love how the teachings are solidified with Scriptures as foundations, and stories and personal testimonies of the author that shows us that yes, they are doable! It is anointed. One can feel the presence and power of the precious Holy Spirit with every chapter and every activation. I know I did! And I'm all excited to share this to our people now! Thank you to my dear brother and friend, Andrew Hopkins, for writing this treasure for the body of Christ. Every believer will greatly benefit from this one."

Hiram G. Pangilinan
Senior Pastor, Church So Blessed
Quezon City, Philippines

More Books by Andrew Hopkins

Carriers of the Ark

Fierce Peace

Expand Your Expression

*An Introduction to Walking in the
Supernatural Power of God*

Clothed with Power

Andrew Hopkins

Clothed With Power: An Introduction to Walking in the Supernatural Power of God

Copyright © 2024 by Andrew Hopkins

ISBN TP: 978-1-7351430-4-0

ISBN HC: 978-1-7351430-6-4

ISBN eBook: 978-1-7351430-5-7

All Scripture quotations, unless otherwise indicated, are taken from the New King James Version®. Copyright © 1982 by Thomas Nelson. Used by permission. All rights reserved.

Scripture quotations marked (NIV) are taken from the Holy Bible, New International Version®, NIV®. Copyright © 1973, 1978, 1984, 2011 by Biblica, Inc.™ Used by permission of Zondervan. All rights reserved worldwide. www.zondervan.com The "NIV" and "New International Version" are trademarks registered in the United States Patent and Trademark Office by Biblica, Inc.™

Scripture quotations marked (NLT) are taken from the Holy Bible, New Living Translation, copyright ©1996, 2004, 2015 by Tyndale House Foundation. Used by permission of Tyndale House Publishers, Carol Stream, Illinois 60188. All rights reserved.

Scripture quotations marked (AMPC) taken from the Amplified® Bible Copyright © 1954, 1958, 1962, 1964, 1965, 1987 by The Lockman Foundation. Used by permission. Lockman.org.

Scripture quotations marked (MSG) are taken from *THE MESSAGE*, copyright © 1993, 2002, 2018 by Eugene H. Peterson. Used by permission of NavPress. All rights reserved. Represented by Tyndale House Publishers, a Division of Tyndale House Ministries.

Scripture quotations marked (NASB) New American Standard Bible®, Copyright © 1960, 1971, 1977, 1995 by The Lockman Foundation. Used by permission. All rights reserved. lockman.org

Scripture quotations marked (TPT) are from The Passion Translation®. Copyright © 2017, 2018, 2020 by Passion & Fire Ministries, Inc. Used by permission. All rights reserved. thepassiontranslation.com.

Italics used for emphasis by the author.

Edited by Abbie and Edie Mourey

Cover and interior design by Christian Rafetto

Published by Breaker Ministries, www.breakerministries.com

Contents

1	**Introduction:** Do it with Everyone, Lord!
5	**Chpt. 1:** Foundation Stones
23	**Chpt. 2:** Why Do We Need Power?
43	**Chpt. 3:** Who is the Holy Spirit?
61	**Chpt. 4:** Speaking in Tongues
79	**Chpt. 5:** Prophesy!
101	**Chpt. 6:** Healing Ministry
117	**Chpt. 7:** Deliverance
137	**Chpt. 8:** Preach the Gospel
157	**Chpt. 9:** The Return of the Ark

Introduction

Do it with Everyone, Lord!

> I am going to send you what my Father has promised; but stay in the city until you have been clothed with power from on high.
>
> Luke 24:49 NIV

In 1921, the renowned healing evangelist, Aimee Semple McPherson, had five weeks of revival in San Diego, California. Being a San Diego native, I was especially intrigued by the history of McPherson's revival services. Before she went on to build the Angelus Temple in Los Angeles and pioneer the Foursquare denomination, she was at the helm of a move of God in San Diego. Starting in a boxing arena, and ending in the outdoor amphitheater in Balboa Park, thousands gave their lives to Jesus, were baptized with the Holy Spirit, and received healing miracles.

The testimonies from the revival are remarkable. A baby that had burned the passage to its stomach by accidentally drinking gasoline, given up to die by doctors, was healed. Another man testified of being completely healed of cataracts that had been growing in his eyes for five years and had hindered him from working. A father shared how his seven grown children had all been saved in the revival, answering years of prayer in a moment. An eighty-two-year-old at the altar was led to the Lord by a teenager. A mother embraced her daughter as her daughter was filled with the Holy Spirit and the gift of tongues came flowing out.

A withered lung, cancer, tuberculosis, tumors—all healed in the name of Jesus. Two deaf and mute sisters heard and spoke for the first time. A young lady who had never walked on her own received healing and walked back to her seat. When she sat down, she realized that she was so occupied with asking Jesus to make her walk that she forgot to ask Him to heal her blind eye. Her mother encouraged her to ask Jesus to heal her while healing was flowing in the room. After prayer, her eye, which had been blind since infancy, opened and she could see!

The power of God was moving so strong that unbelievers were awakened to their need for Jesus. Sister Aimee testified about how a woman, who had given her life to Christ in one of the prior meetings, later brought her fiancé. He was not religious, but after seeing a paralytic get healed—throw his crutches, run, and leap—the woman's fiancé found his way to the altar, kneeling and sobbing.[1]

What an amazing move of God! Wouldn't you want to see that happen again? Wouldn't you want to see that happen in your hometown? While I honor what God did through Sister Aimee and am inspired by the revival, my prayer isn't just, "Do it again, Lord!" My prayer is, "Do it with everyone!"

It was estimated that up to thirty thousand people came through Balboa Park. Sister Aimee and her small team prayed for hundreds[2], but there's no way they could have prayed for thousands, unless they had stayed for weeks and weeks. The size of the crowds was too large for the small number of laborers.

What if, instead of one person laying hands on thirty thousand, we got thirty thousand to lay hands on the world? What if we saw not just a few, but an army of believers walking in power and pointing people to Jesus?

That's what this book is about: equipping the people of God to walk in the power of God.

Look at how the Amplified Bible translates Luke 24:49:

> "Listen carefully: I am sending the Promise of My Father [the Holy Spirit] upon you; but you are to remain in the city [of Jerusalem] until you are clothed (fully equipped) with power from on high."

The Holy Spirit comes to fully equip the Church. According to Jesus, you are fully equipped when you are clothed with the power of God.

In June 2003, I went to a meeting where a prophet named Dick Mills was ministering. He called all the young people ages 8–25 years old to come to the front. He prophesied over all of us saying "These are the warriors for the new millennium." He prophesied that we would walk in signs and wonders, dreams and visions, and gifts and miracles. His style of prophetic ministry was always accompanied by Scriptures, so he gave us a handful of verses to support the prophetic word: Isaiah 8:18; Joel 2:28; Acts 2:22, 5:12; Romans 15:19; 2 Corinthians 12:12; and Hebrews 2:4.

It's been over twenty years since I received that prophetic word, and I can tell you today that I'm walking in *everything* that was prophesied. But now there's a new generation on the rise! Now it's your turn!

This book is an introduction to walking in the supernatural power of God. You'll get sound biblical teaching, inspirational testimonies, and practical activations. Get ready for an upgrade. God wants to clothe you with supernatural power!

Chapter 1

Foundation Stones

> "When constructing a strong, stable building, it all starts with the foundation."
>
> The Constructor

Did you know the Leaning Tower of Pisa wasn't supposed to be leaning? It was meant to be a bell tower but when they got to building the third floor, the building started to lean. Why? Well, in short, because the foundation was faulty.[3]

Let me put it like this: The foundation was not strong enough to support the building's intended purpose.

Keep that in mind.

Let's look at another building: the Burj Khalifa in Dubai. It is the world's tallest building coming in at 2,717 feet high. It took over a year to build the Burj Khalifa's unique and intricate foundation, going 164 feet deep![4]

Why? Because the foundation of any building, organization, or life needs to be strong enough to support the mission or purpose of the thing being built.

Before we dive into walking in power, I want to ensure we understand the need for a strong foundation. A life walked in power needs to be built upon the foundation of a real relationship with Christ.

The thing about foundations is that they are unseen. Yet the unseen foundation provides the house's stability and longevity. In the same way, our foundation in Christ brings stability to our walk in power.

This may be a review for some readers, and it may be new for others. However, we can't talk about walking in power without prioritizing a relationship with Jesus. These foundation stones are what make up healthy and growing disciples of Jesus.

Intimacy with God

> Now this is eternal life: that they know you, the only true God, and Jesus Christ, whom you have sent.
>
> John 17:3 NIV

I love how Jesus defines eternal life in this passage: to know God. This gives us clarity on the true meaning of John 3:16 (NIV): "For God so loved the world that he gave His one and only Son, that whoever believes in Him shall not perish but have eternal life." It's not just about going to heaven one day—although that is indeed a true and wonderful reality—it's about having a relationship with God right now.

It can't be said enough: Christianity is not a religion but a relationship. That's the heart of the gospel. God wants to have a relationship with us, and Jesus' sacrifice made that relationship possible. It's from this relationship that the power of God can flow through us. After healing a crippled man at the pool of Bethesda, Jesus said this: "Most assuredly, I say to you, the Son can do nothing of Himself, but what He sees the Father do; for whatever He does, the Son also does in like manner." (John 5:19). Jesus' life of power was connected to His relationship with His Father. It's the same way for us!

> **It can't be said enough: Christianity is not a religion but a relationship.**

Intimacy has been explained as in-to-me-you-see. In other words, you let God into your heart, and He welcomes you into His. This is what we were created for.

How do you grow your relationship with God? The same way you would with anyone else: spend time with Him. Open your heart to Him. Listen to His word. Receive His love. I've always made a practice of three essential things: worship, prayer, and word.

WORSHIP

> Enter into His gates with thanksgiving, and into His courts with praise. Be thankful to Him, and bless His name.
>
> Psalm 100:4

Take time to sing to the Lord. Take time to thank Him, to praise Him for what He's done. Worship Him for who He is. As you do, your focus gets lifted to Him, and you enter into His Presence. Something supernatural takes place when we sing to the Lord. Psalm 22:3 says, "But You are holy, Enthroned in the praises of Israel". He comes and dwells in our praise.

If you want to experience God's Presence, make it a practice to worship Him. You'll learn to recognize Him when He comes into a room.

PRAYER

All good relationships are built on communication. Prayer and worship are communication from the heart. Open your heart and talk to God. Make this a normal habit to build a friendship with God.

The model prayer Jesus gave us is the Lord's Prayer, which is recorded in Matthew 6:9–13 and Luke 11:1–4. Christians have turned to the Lord's Prayer for centuries as both a guide to prayer and for comfort. I've personally modeled my prayers after the Lord's Prayer and encourage you to do the same.

Here's how I utilize the Lord's Prayer: I take each line of the prayer as a launching point into the topic it presents. For example, "Our Father in heaven, hallowed be your name" speaks of honoring God (Matthew 6:9). So, I start with worship. Then the prayer says, "Your kingdom come, Your will be done, on earth as it is in heaven" (Matthew 6:10). I then pray God's will be done in my life, my family, and all that concerns me.

Another prayer I like to pray consistently is in Ephesians 1:17–19 (NIV): "that the God of our Lord Jesus Christ, the glorious Father, may give you the Spirit of wisdom and revelation, so that you may know Him better. I pray that the eyes of your heart may be enlightened." It's a powerful prayer asking God to reveal Himself to you through the Holy Spirit.

Expect to hear God speak to you. As you do this, things will often come up in your heart as you pray—a Scripture, a word, a direction, or even some things to do that day. Be open to the moving and leading of the Spirit. Prayer is a two-way street of communication!

WORD

> But He answered and said, "It is written, 'Man shall not live by bread alone, but by every word that proceeds from the mouth of God.'"
>
> Matthew 4:4

One of the surest ways to hear God is to read the Bible. Scripture is the written word of God. If you want to be someone who prophesies the word of the Lord, you have to be rooted in Scripture! Scripture reveals the heart of God. If we want to know how God thinks or feels about a matter, we can go to the Word.

Furthermore, Jesus said that God's Word is our food. Just like our bodies are physically sustained by bread, our spiritual lives are sustained by God's Word. I would go even further to say that not just our spiritual lives, but our entire lives—including our physical, mental, and emotional lives—are sustained by God's Word.

Spend time consistently in Scripture. Reading, studying, and meditating are some of the best ways to get to know God.

In all these endeavors, leave space for the Holy Spirit to move. Look for things He's highlighting to you. Listen for His "still small voice" (1 Kings 19:12).

If you sin, repent. If someone wrongs you, forgive. When temptation comes, resist. Walk in love, purity, and kindness. The last thing the kingdom wants or needs are anointed jerks! Staying consistent in our relationships with God keeps us growing in Christlikeness.

Identity in Christ

This subject could be an entire book in itself—but it's so important to know who you are in Christ, especially if you're going to walk in power. In Christ, you are loved, accepted, forgiven, anointed, and empowered.

The issue comes when we try to get our identity from anything other than Christ. We might think our performance can earn what we already have for free in Christ. For example, we might be tempted to think, "If I do miracles, then I will be accepted." But we already have acceptance in Christ. Striving for acceptance becomes exhausting. When you do good, you feel good, but what about when you fall short? You need an identity not built upon your performance.

You also need something steadier than your emotions. There are way too many people in this generation that are getting their identity from their feelings and their thoughts. Just because you "feel" or "think" a certain way, doesn't mean you are what you are feeling.

The world around you will try to define you. Scripture said of Jesus that He was "rejected indeed by men, but chosen by God *and* precious" (1 Peter 2:4). That tells me that Jesus lived with two realities—yet only chose to draw His identity from one: chosen and precious. He didn't go around depressed because He was rejected; instead, He walked in His identity as the chosen Son of God. He had a firm foundation to stand on, even when people around Him rejected Him. We must follow His example.

> **You are who God says you are.**

You are not your performance. You are not your emotions. You are not what the world says you are. *You are who God says you are.* Receive what the Father says about you. Receive the free gift of His love. Our identity is not based on the ever-changing opinions of man. Our identity is rooted in the everlasting truth of God.

One of the best ways to stay rooted in what God says about you is to take the truth of Scripture and declare it over yourself. You can personalize Scripture verses by inserting "I" or "me" wherever "you" appears.

Here are some examples:

If fear comes knocking on your door, trying to get you to live under its influence, declare the truth based out of 2 Timothy 1:7, "God did not give me a spirit of fear, but of power and of love and of a sound mind. I refuse to live by fear! I have the power of God, the love of God, and the mind of Christ!"

If the devil tries to remind you of your past sins, you declare the truth found in Ephesians 1:7, "I am forgiven of my sins because of the riches of God's grace. He's redeemed me through the blood of Jesus!"

If doubt comes against you saying that you're not loved, you get to embrace and declare the truth in Romans 5:8, "God demonstrated His love for me, that even while I was still a sinner, Christ died for me! His cross proves His love for me. I am loved by God."

If thoughts come in saying that you don't have what it takes to walk in power, you can declare with Jesus, "The Spirit of the Lord is upon me, because He has anointed me to preach the gospel to the poor, to heal the broken hearted, to proclaim liberty to the captives and recovery of sight to the blind, and to set free those who are oppressed. I am clothed with power from on high!" (based out of Luke 4:18–19, 24:49; Acts 1:8)

I'd also like to mention the importance of having good character. We want both the *gifts* and the *fruit* of the Holy Spirit (see Galatians 5:22–23). We don't want to be the kind of people who are extremely gifted but lack character.

How disappointing would it be to receive a powerful prophetic word from someone and then that same person goes and gets drunk after the service? How horrible would it be to see someone move in miracles and the next day you hear that they're sleeping around? These things are not right and not who we are as followers of Jesus. Good character flows out of our identity in Christ. We walk in integrity, purity, sobriety, and generosity not because of religious obligation but because *it's who we are*.

Look at how Paul connects good character to our identity in Christ:

> Put to death, therefore, whatever belongs to your earthly nature: sexual immorality, impurity, lust, evil desires and greed, which is idolatry. Because of these, the wrath of God is coming. *You used to walk in these ways, in the life you once lived.* But now you must also rid yourselves of all such things as these: anger, rage, malice, slander, and filthy language from your lips. Do not lie to each other, since *you have taken off your old self with its practices and have put on the new self*, which is being renewed in knowledge in the image of its Creator. Here there is no Gentile or Jew, circumcised or uncircumcised, barbarian, Scythian, slave or free, but Christ is all, and is in all. *Therefore, as God's chosen people, holy and dearly loved, clothe yourselves* with compassion, kindness, humility, gentleness and patience. Bear with each other and forgive one another if any of you has a grievance against someone. Forgive as

the Lord forgave you. And over all these virtues put on love, which binds them all together in perfect unity.

Colossians 3:5–14 NIV

When Jesus died on the cross, He crucified your old sinful nature. Then when He rose up from the grave, He took you with Him and "raised" you up "in newness of life" (Romans 6:4). That's why the Bible calls you a "new creation" (2 Corinthians 5:17). It's from this new identity that we live.

Your identity in Christ can be summed up by the following verse: "So let it be the same way with you! Since you are now joined with Him, you must continually view yourselves as dead and unresponsive to sin's appeal while living daily for God's pleasure in union with Jesus, the Anointed One" (Romans 6:11 TPT).

Take some time to discover who you are in Christ and develop the character of Christ. This provides a solid foundation to walk in Christ's power.

Community

You need to have a local church! A community that seeks God together. Proverbs 18:1 says, "A man who isolates himself seeks his own desire; He rages against all wise judgment." Isolation creates lone rangers. Community brings family. As Psalm 68:6 says, "God sets the lonely in families" (NIV).

When Jesus sent the disciples out to minister the message of the kingdom, He didn't send them as lone rangers. Instead, He sent them two by two. In the same way, a life walked in power should be lived in community with other believers. Find some people who you can pray with, worship God with, and share revelation with. Find people who will spur you on and stir you up to live for Jesus and will help you live in holiness and purity. Find a community that is on fire for the Lord!

I remember driving home from ministering in the Navajo Nation with a few friends. We stopped at a gas station and my friend William spotted a man who grabbed his own shoulder like he was dealing with pain. William said, "Hey, go pray for that guy; he's hurting." I just honestly didn't want to because I was tired, and this man looked like he could take me out if he got angry.

But that didn't stop William. He walked up to the guy and said, "Hey, is your shoulder hurting? I saw you grab it earlier." The man said, "Yes." William told him, "Well, my friend has the gift of healing. You should let him pray for you." I thought to myself, *Well, I wasn't planning on this, but here we go.*

I walked over, greeted him, and prayed. God instantly healed him, and he said, "What the—" I knew he was grateful. The point of this story is to show that I have people who push me past my comfort zone. This is part of what makes a good community!

Find some people that you can have fun with. It's been said that seriousness is not a fruit of the Spirit, but joy is! One thing I love about my community at The Fire & Glory Outpouring in San Diego is the amount of fun we have together. We are on fire for the Lord, but we also have a lot of fun and it's not always about spiritual things. It's random jokes, eating food, talking, and just hanging out, living life together.

One thing that our community does a lot is share testimonies. We hear the wonderful works of God on a regular basis—healings, deliverances, financial breakthroughs, signs and wonders, and all kinds of supernatural things that God has done. God had the people of Israel pass on the testimony of what He had done for them to the next generation. I believe when the Israelites did this, it set the standard for what the next generation could expect from God. Testimonies set the standard and are key to a vibrant community of faith that walks in God's power.

Another thing that is great about community is that you get the opportunity to work with people who annoy you! When Jesus chose His disciples, He put a tax collector and a Zealot on the same team. Zealots wanted to overthrow Rome, and tax collectors worked for Rome. Talk about learning how to love your enemies!

> **Church is training ground for world changers.**

Proverbs 27:17 says, "As iron sharpens iron, so one person sharpens another" (NIV). Sometimes there's friction when iron hits! The disciples, for example, argued with each other about who was the greatest (Mark 9:33–35). Friction works to make communities stronger. How will you learn to love unless you're around people who are hard for you to love?

Church is training ground for world changers. It's the place of encouragement, equipping, correction, healing, and growth. It's one of the best places to practice spiritual gifts.

Authority

God is the ultimate authority, but He's also delegated authority to leaders. They have a grace from God to lead, see the big picture, and "steer the ship." Healthy authority is present to protect you.

Because authority is given by God and exists to protect us, we need to be under leadership. We need to have people who can speak into our lives, to give us encouragement, counsel, direction, and correction when needed. We are not meant to be lone rangers. We are meant to have community around us and leaders above us. The military has leaders, sports teams have leaders, businesses have leaders, families have leaders, and so does the Church.

> Obey your leaders and submit *to them*, for they keep watch over your souls as those who will give an account. Let them do this with joy and not with grief, for this would be unprofitable for you.
>
> Hebrews 13:17 NASB95

I remember many years ago, I was sharing with a friend, who was a leader in my life as well, some of my dreams of traveling ministry. He turned and spoke plainly to me: "Do you even have anyone that is discipling you right now?" I realized I didn't. It was a catalyst moment that made me plug into my local church.

One thing I got from years of being rooted in a local church was discipleship. I had leaders pouring into my life as well as peers to grow with. Discipleship equips you for ministry. I was equipped in prayer, the word, healing ministry, prophetic ministry, evangelism, worship, leadership, and so much more. I received counsel, mentoring, and direction for my life. I was corrected in all kinds of ways too.

These blessings didn't come just because I had community—they also came because I had submitted to authority. I had pastors who could speak into my life. I didn't leave when it got difficult or when there was conflict. I needed to learn to trust my leaders and submit to them even when I disagreed. I had to trust that they loved me and cared for me. It wasn't easy all the time and neither my pastors nor I were perfect—but I needed leaders!

If you look at all the letters that Paul wrote to the churches in the New Testament, they are leadership letters. He's writing as a spiritual father to these communities; giving them praise, correction, doctrine, words from the Lord, and instructions. Paul demonstrates what spiritual authority should look like in the life of a believer.

Many people today say, "I just need God. He's my leader." To be sure, God is the ultimate leader and authority, but God has set up His kingdom with a leadership structure. There are leaders in the body of Christ: apostles, prophets, evangelists, pastors, teachers, and elders who are delegated by God to have authority in the Church and to care for the people. Leaders are there for you!

Submitting to your leaders is one of the best ways to learn humility, servanthood, and selflessness—all vital characteristics for the Christian life.

I realize this topic may bring up the abuses and wounds that some have endured from Church leadership or authority figures in general. There are a few things I would like to say about these abuses. People are not perfect, and they can do messed up things—even in the Church. However, you do not have to live as a victim of others' misconduct for the rest of your life. You have the gift of forgiveness given to you by Christ. Allow God to heal your heart, create healthy boundaries, and embrace God's plan of having leaders in your life. There *are* good leaders out there.

Leadership is there to equip you for the work of the ministry, to disciple you, and to help you become who God made you to be.

I remember one time trying to cast a demon out of this guy at our church. I remember he was snarling as we prayed, almost like an angry dog. This was a new experience for me, so I just started yelling, "In the name of Jesus, come out!" repeatedly. Then my pastor came over and said calmly, "Hey, you don't have to yell, the devil isn't deaf." It was then I began to learn that louder volume doesn't equal greater authority.

It's moments like these when you realize you need leaders if you're going to walk in power.

The Way of Love

> Follow the way of love and eagerly desire gifts of the Spirit, especially prophecy.
>
> 1 Corinthians 14:1 NIV

In the middle of Paul teaching on spiritual gifts in 1 Corinthians, he stops in chapter thirteen and thoroughly describes the attributes of love. Some people completely misinterpret what Paul's saying and say instead, "We just need love," as if it's a replacement for the gifts of the Spirit.

Love is not a *replacement* for the gifts, it's the *way* we should be using the gifts.

Paul says that if you move powerfully in the spiritual gifts but don't have love, the use of the gifts is pointless. Paul said you would be a noisy gong or a clanging cymbal—in other words, annoying. Brian Simmons said, "Gifts without love are a distraction."[5] The last thing we need is people moving in power who are annoying the world instead of reaching the world.

> ❝ If you're going to walk in power, make it your goal to walk in love.

If you're going to walk in power, make it your goal to walk in love. Miracles are a vehicle to get the love of God to people.

Treat people with dignity, kindness, value, and respect. People are not your project; they are people God loves and is trying to get a hold of and bless. Remember, we are representing Jesus.

It's also important to note that love does not equal agreement. You can love someone and yet still disagree with them. It's not hate speech to say that sin is sin. However, it *is* about the way we communicate the message.

I remember a preacher came to the college campus across the street from my church. His preaching was harsh, and he attacked different people groups like Muslims and members of the LGBTQ community. Instead of letting this preacher misrepresent the gospel, I stood up on the ledge next to him and I started preaching.

I told the students that God loved them, and that Jesus died for them. Guess what? They all started cheering! What was the difference? Love.

Look at this description of love:

> Love is patient, love is kind. It does not envy, it does not boast, it is not proud. It does not dishonor others, it is not self-seeking, it is not easily angered, it keeps no record of wrongs. Love does not delight in evil but rejoices with the truth.
>
> 1 Corinthians 13:4–6 NIV

I love the way the Amplified Classic Bible translates verse seven:

> Love bears up under anything *and* everything that comes, is ever ready to believe the best of every person, its hopes are

fadeless under all circumstances, and it endures everything [without weakening].

1 Corinthians 13:7 AMPC

Wow! That's the love of God. This is what we get to bring to the world around us. Follow the way of love as you walk in power.

How's Your Foundation?

Let's recap.

Five important foundation stones:

1. Intimacy with God
2. Identity in Christ
3. Community
4. Authority
5. The Way of Love

You are reading this book because you want to walk in the power of God. As quoted at the beginning of this chapter, "When constructing a strong, stable building, it all starts with the foundation."[6] Make sure your foundation is solid.

Activations

Out of these five stones, what are the ones you really need to put in place? Here are some activations for each stone:

- Intimacy with God: Make time to spend with God. Find a place and time that works for you. An easy starting place is ten minutes in worship, ten minutes in prayer, ten minutes in the word every day. Then grow from there.
- Identity in Christ: Search the Scriptures for five statements that God makes about you. Turn these statements into declarations and speak them over yourself daily.
- Community: Find a local church and get connected. Find some people who are on fire for Jesus. Join a ministry team and start serving.
- Authority: Let your leaders know that you are open to their leadership in your life. Serve their vision and honor their authority in your life.
- The Way of Love: Read through and meditate on 1 Corinthians 13:4–8. Ask God to fill you with His love and highlight an aspect of love to focus on for the week. Look for ways to implement that kind of love.

For more on becoming a person who carries the Presence of God, I recommend my book *Carriers of the Ark*.

Chapter 2

Why Do We Need Power?

> Most of what is recognized as Christian lifestyle can be accomplished by people who don't even know God.
>
> Bill Johnson, *When Heaven Invades Earth*

If you were to take a quick survey of people and ask them, "How would you describe Christian people?" you might get answers like: "They're religious," "They're right-wing, pro-life, Republicans," or "They're nice people who do good things." You probably wouldn't hear people describe Christians as "Those are the people who walk in power!"

Think about it. You don't need the power of God to help an old lady cross the street, but you do need the power of God to take her hip and back pain away so she can walk for herself. Even in the Old Testament, Moses told God, "If your Presence does not go with us, do not send us up from here...What else will *distinguish* me and your people from all the other people on the face of the earth?" (Exodus 33:15–16 NIV). Moses knew it was the supernatural Presence of God that would set the Israelites apart. How much more do we need this understanding in the Church today?

The power of God sets us apart! We don't want to be known for what everyone else can do. We want to be known for the things that only people who know God can do!

Miracles were one of the things that set Jesus apart from everyone else. He was the first one in all of history to open the eyes of the blind (John 9:32). He cast out demons, made the lame walk, cleansed the lepers, raised the dead, and healed every kind of sickness and disease. These were the signs of the Messiah, the long-awaited King who would come and rescue His people. By these signs, the Israelites would distinguish the Messiah from an imposter. Jesus is still proving He is the Messiah today through miracles, signs, and wonders.

Our King showed up, preached the kingdom of God, and demonstrated His kingdom. When healing came, the kingdom came. When deliverance came, the kingdom came. The mission was "on earth as it is in heaven" (Matthew 6:10).

It was the same for the disciples: power was part of their reputation. Jesus commissioned the disciples in Matthew 10:7–8 saying, "And as you go, preach, saying, 'The kingdom of heaven is at hand.' Heal the sick, cleanse the lepers, raise the dead, cast out demons. Freely you have received, freely give." The disciples continued the ministry of the kingdom.

Acts 5:15–16 says, "As a result, people brought the sick into the streets and laid them on beds and mats so that at least Peter's shadow might fall on some of them as he passed by. Crowds gathered also from the towns around Jerusalem, bringing their sick and those tormented by impure spirits, and all of them were healed" (NIV).

The ministry of power continues today. Jesus is still showing Himself as Messiah by moving through His people. This is what we were meant to do! We were made to walk in power.

Let's take a closer look at why we need the power of God.

Jesus Said It

> But you shall receive power when the Holy Spirit has come upon you; and you shall be witnesses to Me in Jerusalem, and in all Judea and Samaria, and to the end of the earth.
>
> Acts 1:8

The disciples spent years with Jesus, so you would think they would be qualified and ready to preach the gospel. After all, the disciples saw Jesus do miracles, and the disciples did miracles themselves. They got the inside scoop on the kingdom, the meanings of the parables, and had a unique friendship with Jesus.

Yet, after Jesus died and resurrected, He appeared to them, and told the disciples to go and preach the gospel. Before they went, however, they had to wait for the power of the Holy Spirit to come upon them.

This reveals an important facet of the Christian life. Before you go out and preach the gospel, you need to receive the power of the Holy Spirit. If this was true for the *most qualified* disciples, how much more for us? When Jesus was speaking to the disciples about their need for the power of God, He was also speaking to us.

The apostle Paul believed in the power of God too. When he went to Corinth to preach, he described his ministry like this:

> My message and my preaching were not with wise and persuasive words, but with a *demonstration of the Spirit's power*, so that your faith might not rest on human wisdom, but on God's power.
>
> 1 Corinthians 2:4–5 NIV

Our faith is meant to rest on the power of God. But if the power of God never shows up, how are people supposed to have faith the way God wants them to? I'd rather do ministry the way God intended: full of the power of the Holy Spirit.

One of the ways that the power Jesus spoke of in Acts 1:8 showed up was through miracles. The healing of the cripple at the Gate Beautiful, people healed and delivered through Peter's shadow, the dead raised, and the various other miracles recorded in the gospels and Acts display the power of the Holy Spirit. And of course, the greatest miracle is people receiving the gift of salvation and becoming born again.

One time I was doing a livestream service on Zoom for a church and God pointed a young lady out to me. Through a word of knowledge, I saw her playing sports and asked if she did so. She told me she did but could no longer play because she had developed iron deficiency anemia which caused lethargy.

I realized I was in a God-ordained moment. Just a week before I was talking with some friends about another young man who had been healed of anemia! I briefly shared this man's testimony and prayed for her healing; her mother prayed as well.

A month later the report came that she had stopped taking her medications believing she had been healed. After a blood test, it was revealed that her iron levels were normal! This miracle was the result of the power Jesus spoke of in Acts 1:8.

If we want to live as Jesus lived, we need the same power source Jesus had.

Jesus Walked in Power

Every denomination believes that believers are called to be like Jesus. That's why the WWJD, "What Would Jesus Do," acronym is still floating around out there. We all agree that Jesus is the standard. So, if Jesus is the one we're following, we ought to follow Him into a life of power.

> **If Jesus walked in power, then it would only follow suit that His followers should also walk in power.**

If the followers don't live like the leader, then the followers aren't following that well! But by the grace of God, we can live like Jesus.

Jesus said this, "Very truly I tell you, whoever believes in me will do the works I have been doing, and they will do even greater things than these, because I am going to the Father" (John 14:12 NIV).

Jesus said we can do the same things He did! And even greater things. Look at how Matthew described the miracles Jesus performed:

> And Jesus went about all Galilee, teaching in their synagogues, preaching the gospel of the kingdom, and healing all kinds of sickness and all kinds of disease among the people. Then His fame went throughout all Syria; and they brought

to Him all sick people who were afflicted with various diseases and torments, and those who were demon-possessed, epileptics, and paralytics; and He healed them.

Matthew 4:23–24

Acts 10:38 describes Jesus' life like this, "How God anointed Jesus of Nazareth with the Holy Spirit and with power, who went about doing good and healing all who were oppressed by the devil, for God was with Him."

If Jesus walked in power, then it would only follow suit that His followers should also walk in power. The goal is for people to see Jesus in His followers.

Bill Johnson explains what it is to be a witness for God: "To give witness is to 'represent.' This actually means to *re-present* Him. Therefore, to re-present Him without power is a major shortcoming. It is impossible to give an adequate witness of God without demonstrating His supernatural power."[7]

I remember one time ministering to a young girl who had a spirit of suicide. Her eyes were rolling in the back of her head as the demon was trying to take over. I asked her if there was anyone she needed to forgive and she ended up forgiving an ex-boyfriend. When she forgave him, we commanded the spirit to go, and the evil spirit left her. She then received the Holy Spirit and the gift of tongues!

Isn't it amazing how God is still using His people to bring healing and freedom? Jesus continues His ministry today through His people!

The Christian Life is a Supernatural Life

Human beings are spiritual beings. When Paul was correcting the Corinthians for their immature behavior, he essentially told them, "You are acting like mere humans" (see 1 Corinthians 3:3 NIV). Paul's statement makes it very clear that humans are not just physical entities. We have a spiritual nature as well.

There's more to us than our physical and biological makeup. Yes, we are human beings. We're not gods or angels. This being said, we have a spiritual nature that too often gets overlooked. The Christian life is not another religious option that gives you a way to be a better human. The Christian life is a supernatural life!

A brief survey through the Gospels and book of Acts will show all kinds of supernatural phenomena happening: angels visiting, demons being cast out, extraordinary miracles, healings of bodies, laws of nature overridden, the dead being raised, trances, visions, prophecies, and much more. This list of miracles doesn't even include those of the Old Testament, such as the parting of the Red Sea, a visible cloud and pillar of fire that accompanied Israel in the desert, the walls of a city crumbling at a shout, and again, many others.

The people of God have always been a supernatural people because we have a supernatural God.

In Acts 12, the church is praying, and God sends an angel to set Peter free from prison. When he comes to the door, the servant girl who heard his knocking gets so excited that Peter is there that she forgets to let him in. She runs and tells the others in the house, and this is their response:

> "You're out of your mind," they told her. When she kept insisting that it was so, they said, "It must be his angel."
>
> Acts 12:15 NIV

There's a lot that could be said here, but the point I want to make is that their reason for not believing the servant girl was that it "must be his angel." This tells me that they had way more of a supernatural culture than we often realize. In other words, it was normal for them to expect angels to interact with them. If you say that in most churches today, you'd be the weird person. But to the believers in Acts, God's help coming through angels was normal.

The normal Christian life is supernatural! We are spiritual people!

Unfortunately, the supernatural is too far removed from corporate Christianity today. The power of God is uncommon in many churches. We've forgotten who we are. The supernatural is our inheritance. Don't give any room for a spirit of religion to grow! We can be naturally supernatural.

We might be tempted to think, "We don't want to freak out the new people." But don't we want to introduce people to the fullness of who God really is, instead of a mild, watered-down version?

Look at what Paul says about a church that embraces prophecy, "But if an unbeliever or an inquirer comes in while everyone is prophesying, they are convicted of sin and are brought under judgment by all, as the secrets of their hearts are laid bare. So they will fall down and worship God, exclaiming, 'God is really among you!'" (1 Corinthians 14:24–25 NIV). These are the types of experiences that should be commonplace in our churches!

I remember leading at my church's young adult group years ago. I was about to close the service when a flash came to mind. The image was of a right leg. I told everyone, "I'm going to go out on a limb here and ask is there anyone here with pain in their right leg?" A bit of awkward silence passed until a guy on the right side of the room raised his hand. I commissioned some guys around him to pray for him and that young man was healed.

Here's what I found out after the service ended. As we were talking, the young man told me that he had prayed earlier. I had been leading worship at the beginning of the service, and he looked at me and prayed in his heart saying, "God, tell that guy that my leg hurts." And literally right before I ended the service, I called him out and God healed Him! Then he dedicated his life to Jesus right there.

On another occasion, someone brought their cousin to a service where I was ministering and at the end of the service, I prayed and prophesied over this cousin. I later found out that the young man was shocked that I knew so much about him because I had never met him before!

The supernatural should be normal for followers of Jesus. Jesus said that signs would follow those who believe. In the New Testament, it wasn't just the twelve apostles that walked in power, it was all the disciples. The seventy in Luke 10 were commissioned by the Lord to heal the sick. People like Stephen, who became the first martyr, did not carry the title of apostle. He was a regular disciple, yet the Bible said he was "full of faith and the Holy Spirit" and did "great signs and wonders among the people" (Acts 6:5, 8).

Don't settle for a Christianity that has no power. Don't settle for a form of godliness that denies God's power (see 2 Timothy 3:5). The culture set forth in the New Testament tells us that the Christian life is a supernatural life.

Power Shows that God is Real

Jesus said we would receive power to be His witness. A witness is defined as "a person or thing that affords evidence."[8] When people wonder if God is real, we can give them supernatural evidence of His power working through our lives.

I remember ministering in Northern Canada with my friend Jerame Nelson. I was leading worship, and as Jerame got up, he prayed for a man who needed healing in his blood. I watched as Jerame waved his hand and released the fire of God and this man fell to the ground. We went on with the service as usual as these kinds of manifestations are normal to us.

A couple of days later, we were in another city ministering. The same guy from the other meeting found out where we were ministering and drove down. He walked into the service we were at with a paper in his hand that he wanted to show Jerame. It was a doctor's report of a blood test that said he was totally healed of HIV/AIDS! Praise God!

The story gets better. This man apparently was a leader in the drug ring in his region and when God touched him, he repented, and his repentance began to upend the drug trafficking in that area! All because of one miracle.

Only God can do this kind of stuff! Power provides evidence for the reality of God. In the San Diego revival that Aimee Semple McPherson hosted in 1921, Sister Aimee testified of a distinguished-looking man who said, "The miracles which I have seen in this meeting convince me of the reality of a living God." With tears in his eyes, he said, "I want to be a Christian. I must be saved today."[9]

Miracles are one of the things God uses to cause people to repent. What is repentance? The changing of the mind and turning away from one's sin. God uses miracles to change people's minds about Him.

This is what Jesus did in His earthly ministry, as the following verses show,

> Then He began to rebuke the cities in which most of His mighty works had been done, because they did not repent: "Woe to you, Chorazin! Woe to you, Bethsaida! For if the mighty works which were done in you had been done in Tyre and Sidon, they would have repented long ago in sackcloth and ashes.
>
> Matthew 11:20–21

It's interesting that Jesus rebukes the cities that did not repent once they saw the miracles. This tells us that Jesus' objective in doing miracles was repentance. The proper response to miracles is repentance.[10] Now, miracles aren't a guarantee that people will believe, but they do reveal God's existence. People always have a choice about what they will do with what they have seen.

> **" Demonstrating the supernatural power of God is one of the best ways to show that God exists.**

It is as if every miracle proclaims, "God is real, and God is here! There's a greater kingdom here! It's time to change your mind about everything. The Messiah is here!"

When people get touched with the reality of God, it has the potential to upend their entire way of life and transform their lives into what God always meant for them to look like! Isn't that what happened when God revealed Himself to you? You began to change the way you thought about everything. That's repentance: changing the way you think.

People need to know that God is real. Demonstrating the supernatural power of God is one of the best ways to show that God exists.

Power Shows God's Love

Miracles are a vehicle to bring God's love to people.

I remember I was preaching at a youth conference in Colorado once, and God showed me that He wanted to heal someone's right ear. There was a young guy there who had undergone multiple surgeries on his ear and suffered from terrible hearing most of his life. He was even wearing a hearing aid at the event. But when we prayed for him, he said his ear popped open and he could hear perfectly.

More recently, I was praying for a young lady who was dealing with scoliosis and God began to move. She started moving her back in ways she was not able to before and the tears just streamed down her face. That's the love of God!

In the Bible, one leper bravely made his way to Jesus and begged Him for healing. The leper said to Jesus, "If You are willing, You can make me clean" (Mark 1:40).

Imagine being a leper in Jesus' day. Quarantined from society, you couldn't even be close to your loved ones, and if people came near you, you were supposed to cry out, "Unclean!" Not to mention the physical trauma of this horrible disease eating away at your body. It was a lonely, degrading, and depressing experience.

> Then Jesus, moved with compassion, stretched out His hand and touched him, and said to him, "I am willing; be cleansed." As soon as He had spoken, immediately the leprosy left him, and he was cleansed.
>
> Mark 1:41–42

Not only was this man's body restored, but his entire life was transformed. Jesus touched him. He hadn't experienced human touch for who knows how long. A season of rejection shifted in a moment. Think of the healing this man's heart experienced at the same time his body was healed. He could be restored back to his family, back to his job, back to his people. The power of God came with the love of God.

Whether it's a healing miracle, a prophetic word, a word of knowledge—whatever it is—the power of God brings the love of God to people.

God cares about people. Multiple times in the Gospels, Scripture says that Jesus was moved with compassion, and from that place, He ministered healing (Matthew 14:14, 20:34; Luke 7:13).

But it's not just healing ministry. It's really the Presence of God that changes everything. God is omnipresent—which means He is everywhere at all times. But He's not always manifest present—which is when He reveals Himself in a felt way. That's what we're after.

Sometimes the Holy Spirit just comes, and His Presence alone is enough. The fact that He is near and felt brings relief. His Presence sets everything in order. I've heard stories of hugs that felt so anointed they set people free. God is love and so if He manifests His Presence, we are stepping into the presence of the purest, greatest, and holiest love.

When we carry the Presence and power of God, people experience the love of God. His love is supernatural. His love is life changing. Psalm 63:3 says, His "love is better than life" (NIV). His love is what every human on the planet is craving.

Experiencing God's love should not just be something people read about in Scripture. People need to experience His love as well. Paul calls this "the most excellent way" (1 Corinthians 12:31 NIV).

When we're filled with the Holy Spirit, we become the conduits for this love to flow through us to the world around us.

The Baptism of the Holy Spirit

> I indeed baptize you with water unto repentance, but He who is coming after me is mightier than I, whose sandals I am not worthy to carry. He will baptize you with the Holy Spirit and fire.
>
> John the Baptist, Matthew 3:11

How do you step into this life of power? You need the baptism in the Holy Spirit and fire!

Salvation is just the beginning. If salvation is joining the army, then the baptism in the Holy Spirit is receiving your weapons and gear for battle—getting fully equipped. When you believed in Jesus, God forgave your sins, made you a new person, and sent the Holy Spirit to dwell within you. But the baptism in the Holy Spirit is a separate experience from salvation that empowers you to be a witness for Christ.

The original disciples had a born-again experience when Jesus breathed on them, and they received the Holy Spirit (John 20:22). Similarly, God breathed the breath of life into Adam, and he became a living being (Genesis 2:7). But the disciples still needed the Holy Spirit to empower them for ministry.

> And being assembled together with them, He commanded them not to depart from Jerusalem, but to wait for the Promise of the Father, "which," He said, "you have heard from Me; for John truly baptized with water, but you shall be baptized with the Holy Spirit not many days from now."
>
> Acts 1:4–5

If they needed to be baptized with the Holy Spirit, how much more do we need this baptism?

The purpose of the baptism in the Holy Spirit is power; power that points people to Jesus. Jesus said, "But you will receive power when the Holy Spirit comes on you; and you will be my witnesses in Jerusalem, and in all Judea and Samaria, and to the ends of the earth" (Acts 1:8 NIV).

In Luke 24:49, Jesus says, "I am going to send you what my Father has promised; but stay in the city until you have been clothed with power from on high" (NIV).

The Greek word for "power" in these passages is *dunamis*.[11] Dunamis is where we get our English word "dynamite." It speaks of the dynamic, explosive, supernatural, miracle-working power of God! It speaks of God's ability.

God wants to clothe us with His ability!

God fulfilled His promise when the disciples were waiting and praying in the upper room,

> When the day of Pentecost came, they were all together in

one place. Suddenly a sound like the blowing of a violent wind came from heaven and filled the whole house where they were sitting. They saw what seemed to be tongues of fire that separated and came to rest on each of them. All of them were filled with the Holy Spirit and began to speak in other tongues as the Spirit enabled them.

Acts 2:1–4 NIV

Look what happened next,

Now there were staying in Jerusalem God-fearing Jews from every nation under heaven. When they heard this sound, a crowd came together in bewilderment, because each one heard their own language being spoken. Utterly amazed, they asked:

"Aren't all these who are speaking Galileans? Then how is it that each of us hears them in our native language?"

Acts 2:5–8 NIV

What a miracle! The Holy Spirit gave the disciples the ability to speak in languages they never learned before and this captured the attention of the crowds. Then Peter took the opportunity to preach the gospel and 3,000 people gave their lives to Jesus that day (Acts 2:14–41)! The disciples went on to walk in the supernatural ministry of Jesus. They truly were clothed with power.

The baptism in the Holy Spirit unlocks everything. A life of miracles, healings, the reality of God, the love of God—a life that produces supernatural evidence of the Lord Jesus Christ—is unleashed through the power of the Spirit.

One minister said he prayed for around 900 people to be healed and no one got healed. But when he received the baptism in the Holy Spirit and fire, people began to get healed! We can't do this without His power. We *need* the baptism of the Holy Spirit!

Have you received the baptism in the Holy Spirit? Are you ready to be clothed with power from on high? Get ready for the upgrade! He's about to shift you out of a powerless Christianity and into a life of supernatural power that points people to Jesus. If you want to make an impact on the world for Christ, you need the baptism in the Holy Spirit and fire!

And if you've already received the baptism, there's more! The same disciples that were filled in Acts 2 got filled again in Acts 4:31. Paul said in Ephesians 5:18 "be filled continually with the Holy Spirit" (TPT).

Now is the time to step into a life of power. Now is the time for a fresh baptism in the Holy Spirit!

Activation

I want to lead you to receive the baptism of the Holy Spirit.

Things to know about the baptism of the Holy Spirit:

- The baptism is for believers.
  - If you're not a follower of Jesus and you want to be, you can turn from your sins right now, accept His gift of forgiveness, and give your life to Him through prayer. Call on Jesus to save you!
- The baptism is all about Jesus.
  - Jesus said we will receive power when the Holy Spirit comes upon us, and we will then be His witnesses. That means your life should point to Jesus.
- The baptism's purpose is power.
  - The most common manifestation when people are baptized in the Holy Spirit is speaking in tongues; however, the purpose of the baptism is not tongues. The purpose for the baptism is that we would walk in God's power. I will speak more about the gift of tongues later in this book. For now, just receive the gift!

The purpose of the baptism in the Holy Spirit is to give you power to produce supernatural evidence that points to Jesus.

Receive the baptism of the Holy Spirit:

- Be open to and hungry for the Holy Spirit and His gifts.
- Ask! Cry out! Scripture tells us to ask God for the gift of the Spirit.

- ○ "If you then, though you are evil, know how to give good gifts to your children, how much more will your Father in heaven give the Holy Spirit to those who ask him!" (Luke 11:13 NIV)
- Receive the baptism of the Holy Spirit by faith.

You may want to ask someone who's filled with the Holy Spirit to lay hands on you and pray. That's how the baptism of the Holy Spirit happened in the book of Acts,

> Then Peter and John placed their hands on them, and they received the Holy Spirit.
>
> Acts 8:17 NIV

> When Paul had laid hands on them, the Holy Spirit came upon them, and they spoke with tongues and prophesied.
>
> Acts 19:6 NIV

Here's a sample prayer. Open your hands and pray,

"Father God, I need Your power. So, Jesus, baptize me with the Holy Spirit and fire. Come, Holy Spirit, and fill me up. Clothe me with power from on high. I receive the *dunamis* power of the Holy Spirit so I can be a witness for Jesus. Baptize me, Lord!"

Expect power to come upon you now. Receive it!

You may begin speaking in a new language. Just let it flow.

You may physically feel the Presence of God come on you as a sensation of heat, tingling, or weight. You may even begin to cry. No matter what, just receive by faith the gift of the Holy Spirit.

Receive the baptism of the Spirit! Receive the fire, in Jesus' name, amen!

Chapter 3

Who is the Holy Spirit?

> The amazing grace of the Master, Jesus Christ, the extravagant love of God, the intimate friendship of the Holy Spirit, be with all of you.
>
> 2 Corinthians 13:14 MSG

Years ago, when I was leading my church's young adult group, whenever I would preach about the Holy Spirit, I would emphasize His power. A friend approached me and graciously told me, "You know, there's more to the Holy Spirit than just power," and he referred to how Jesus spoke of the Holy Spirit in John 14–16. Now, whenever people come and criticize your preaching, there's a little insecurity that tries to rise up, but I knew he was right.

This situation helped me to see even more that the Holy Spirit was a Person that I could have a relationship with. One of my pastors gave me a book about another minister's relationship with the Holy Spirit and I couldn't put it down. The Holy Spirit would encounter me even as I read this book. The author's genuine relationship with the Spirit oozed through the pages.

I asked the Lord, "Do I even know the Holy Spirit?" And one by one, He began bringing up memories of when I had encountered His Presence. All these encounters in personal times of worship and church services had been the Holy Spirit coming and revealing Himself to me. Through those encounters, I developed a friendship with the Holy Spirit without even realizing it.

I watched Bill Johnson speak so tenderly of the Holy Spirit in a documentary and it marked me. All he did was quote Jesus saying that He is the "Promise of [the] Father" but there was so much depth to it (Luke 24:49). His words carried with them an uncommon intimacy with God.[12]

This whole experience inspired my song "Ode to the Spirit."

> "You're the Promise of the Father
> You're the Comforter of man
> You're the Spirit of the grace of God
> and how can I begin…
> To say that
> I love You
> I need You
> My closest friend
> Holy Spirit, come."[13]

I learned that a relationship with the Holy Spirit is vital to a life in Christ. The Holy Spirit is not just some force we use to do miracles, He is God! God is three-in-one: Father, Son, and Spirit. The Spirit is just as much God as the Father and the Son are.

I want to take an entire chapter to discuss the Person of the Holy Spirit. As we step into a life of power, with the Spirit being the one who empowers us, we would do well to get to know Him.

The Holy Spirit is a Person

The Holy Spirit is a Person you can have a relationship with. It's so important to realize this. He's not an "it." He's not a "force." He's a Person! He's the very Person of God. And as a Person, He's relational. He wants a friendship with you.

The Holy Spirit speaks to us.

> Then *the Spirit said* to Philip, "Go near and overtake this chariot.
>
> Acts 8:29

> As they ministered to the Lord and fasted, *the Holy Spirit said*, "Now separate to Me Barnabas and Saul for the work to which I have called them."
>
> Acts 13:2

As a Person, the Holy Spirit can be grieved.

> And *do not grieve the Holy Spirit* of God, by whom you were sealed for the day of redemption.
>
> Ephesians 4:30

And as a Person, you can please the Holy Spirit.

> For it seemed good to the Holy Spirit, and to us.
>
> Acts 15:28

All of these are relational qualities. As you grow in relationship with anyone, you learn their voice—the tones in their voice and what they mean. You learn what makes that person happy, and what makes them sad. You learn what's important to them and what moves them. And when you understand those things, you do what you can do to maintain connection with that person.

You don't do things that would hurt or sadden the person you love. You look for ways to connect with them and make them feel valuable. You don't want to grieve a person you love; you want to please that person. Not because you're a people pleaser, but because you want to maintain a genuine connection. You want a good relationship. This is how it should be with the Holy Spirit. This is what Jesus came to give us: a living relationship with a living God.

You learn what pleases and grieves the Holy Spirit through Scripture and spending time with Him. The Scripture is full of what pleases God and what grieves God. Just look at the following verses after Paul says to not grieve the Spirit,

> Get rid of all bitterness, rage, anger, harsh words, and slander, as well as all types of evil behavior. Instead, be kind to each other, tenderhearted, forgiving one another, just as God through Christ has forgiven you.
>
> Ephesians 4:31–32 NLT

Here, and elsewhere in Scripture, we have clear instructions on what will hurt our connection with the Spirit and what will help our connection with the Spirit.

One of the things that Jesus said the Holy Spirit would do is convict us of sin. "And when He has come, He will convict the world of sin, and of righteousness, and of judgment" (John 16:8). I've experienced this in at least two ways. When I'm tempted in any area to sin, or if I have sinned, I feel His grief within me. I feel convicted that I did something wrong or am about to do something wrong. Sometimes I will have a Scripture come to mind that clearly tells me what is right and what is wrong. In those moments, I can repent, change my ways, change directions, and move away from sin. I get to turn from sin and into righteousness. All of these are part of maintaining connection with Him. The goal is relationship.

> **The Holy Spirit is a Person you can have a relationship with.**

There is another voice, however, that tries to come alongside the voice of conviction. It's the voice of condemnation. Conviction is when the Holy Spirit tells you that you did something wrong or are about to do something wrong. He helps us just like a loving father would let his child know they're about to do something destructive. Conversely, condemnation tells you that you're condemned. It tries to make an identity out of your sin or temptation.

Conviction tells you that you did something wrong, condemnation tells you that you are something wrong. Conviction will point you in the right direction, condemnation will heap shame and guilt on you. Conviction is the voice of a loving father; condemnation is the voice of a destructive enemy. Follow the voice of the Spirit!

The Holy Spirit is a Person who can be experienced. As with any relationship, experience is required. You can experience the Person of the Holy Spirit. It's only then that you begin to understand what the psalmists meant when they said, "How lovely is Your dwelling place...better is one day in Your courts than a thousand elsewhere...I love the house where you live, the place where Your glory dwells" (Psalm 26:8; 84:1, 10 NIV). These writings are not just poetry, metaphors, or theories. This is what living with the Holy Spirit is like!

The psalmists wrote this way because they experienced Holy Spirit. They felt Him. They stepped into Him. He surrounded them. They experienced the life that flows from His Presence. They found something in Him they couldn't get anywhere else: ultimate satisfaction in the Presence of God.

The Presence of God, the Holy Spirit revealing Himself, is life itself. His Presence is better than a thousand vacations, all the money in the world, all the fame, all the earthly pleasures. He's the goal of life. He's the atmosphere of peace. He's everything we've ever wanted. Many of us have heard that everyone has a God-shaped hole in their hearts that can only be filled with God.[14] Augustine sums it up so well in his prayer to God, "Our hearts are restless until they rest in You."[15]

Miracles are great, and the focus of this book is activating a generation to walk in power, but intimacy with the Lord is what we're made for. It's the foundation and life source for not just a walk of power, but also life itself. Jesus is better than everything.

When David sinned against God, he didn't say, "Don't take the kingdom from me...don't take my riches." He said, "Don't take Your Holy Spirit from me" (Psalm 51:11). The most precious thing to David was the Presence of the Holy Spirit. May it be the same way with us.

The Holy Spirit is a Person, and you can experience Him.

The Holy Spirit is Our Helper

> But the Comforter (Counselor, Helper, Intercessor, Advocate, Strengthener, Standby), the Holy Spirit, Whom the Father will send in My name.
>
> John 14:26 AMPC

When Jesus spoke of the Holy Spirit, the Greek word He used is *Parakletos*.[16] It means someone who is called alongside to help. The word is often translated as "comforter" or "helper," but the Amplified Bible uses seven English words listed above to describe the role of the Holy Spirit.

> **The Holy Spirit ministers in our lives. He brings comfort, counsel, and help.**

The Holy Spirit ministers in our lives. He brings comfort, counsel, and help. He prays for us, speaks for us, strengthens us, and is an "ever-present help in trouble" (Psalm 46:1 NIV). I believe He's present not just to help us with "spiritual" matters, but with the entirety of our lives!

Let's look at a few ways the Holy Spirit helps us.

PRAYER

I don't always know what to pray for, but the Holy Spirit does. I may think I know what to pray for, and I can still pray using my own reason or understanding, but He always knows best. When you follow the leading of the Spirit, He'll take you places you would not have come to on your own. He'll begin to bring up people, places, or things you need to pray for, He'll bring up Scriptures He wants to talk to you about, He'll give you vision for the road ahead, and so much more.

I'll go more in-depth on tongues in a later chapter, but I pray in tongues more than I pray in English. When we pray in tongues, the Holy Spirit is praying perfect prayers through us. While I'm praying, things begin to come up in my mind or heart, much like the notifications that come up on my smartphone. The Holy Spirit begins to bring up things that I need to attend to. It could be spiritual things such as sermon ideas, songs for a service, or prophetic words, but the Holy Spirit can also remind me of practical things to do like, "Take the trash out," "update the schedule," or "text someone back."

In other words, I treat prayer like a conversation, not a monologue. I expect to hear from the Holy Spirit. I expect to receive His leading. And I'm so grateful that He speaks! Almost everything I do in ministry comes from times of prayer.

STRENGTH

Paul prayed in Ephesians 3:16 "that He would grant you, according to the riches of His glory, to be strengthened with might through His Spirit in the inner man." The Holy Spirit strengthens us.

He gives us strength to face adversity. The enemy wants to sap us of our strength through fear, discouragement, shame, temptations, accusations, and persecution. God, however, wants to give us strength by His Spirit. Paul said in Colossians 1:11 MSG, "We pray that you'll have the strength to stick it out over the long haul—not the grim strength of gritting your teeth but the glory-strength God gives. It is strength that endures the unendurable."

It's supernatural, heavenly strength. It's the kind of strength that causes you to rise above your circumstances, instead of your circumstances ruling your life. It's the strength that causes us to shake off the gloominess of depression and discouragement and run the race with perseverance.

I've also found that the Holy Spirit strengthens me to meet the demands of ministry. Look at what Colossians 1:29 AMPC says: "For this I labor [unto weariness], striving with all the superhuman energy which He so mightily enkindles and works within me." There have been times where I've done so many services in a weekend that, naturally, I should not have had the energy to do them. But praise God for the anointing of the Holy Spirit because through His power I have been able to complete these services!

The anointing of the Holy Spirit can make you feel superhuman. There have been times I have been physically tired along with my voice losing strength, but when the anointing came upon me I was able to do all that I needed to do with strength, energy, and clarity!

ENCOURAGEMENT

Sometimes it helps to think of the Holy Spirit like a coach. A good coach is always encouraging you, calling you higher, and telling you who you truly are. A good coach is an advocate for his team. Similarly, the Holy Spirit is the Advocate who speaks for you!

He's an encouraging friend like Barnabas. Barnabas' real name was Joseph, but he earned the nickname Barnabas, which means "son of encouragement" (Acts 4:36 NIV). Barnabas spoke up for the apostle Paul when no one believed him because of his past (Acts 9:27).

The Holy Spirit testifies to us about what Jesus did for us at the cross. He will relay the victory of the cross to us: God demonstrated His love for us, our debt has been paid for, our sins have been forgiven, and we've been redeemed (see Hebrews 10:15–17).

The Holy Spirit is the embodiment of "God is for you" (Romans 8:31). He will tell it like it is and correct you when you need it. The Holy Spirit will always remind you of who you truly are, and what Jesus accomplished for you.

Ask God for the help and strength of the Holy Spirit!

The Holy Spirit is the Revealer

Here is a familiar passage that doesn't always get quoted in context:

But as it is written:

> "Eye has not seen, nor ear heard, nor have entered into the heart of man the things which God has prepared for those who love Him."
>
> 1 Corinthians 2:9

And most people stop right there.

But the next verse is so powerful. "But God has revealed them to us through His Spirit." It goes on to say: "Now we have received, not the spirit of the world, but the Spirit who is from God, that we might know the things that have been freely given to us by God" (1 Corinthians 2:10,12).

One of the Holy Spirit's jobs in our lives is to reveal to us the truth and wisdom of God. He wants to give you prophetic insight (John 16:13).

Revelation is the Holy Spirit showing you things you've never seen before. These things have always been there, but you haven't seen them yet. And when God speaks and reveals, it's life-giving! It's enlightening! It's not just head knowledge, its experience, encounter, and heart knowledge. You don't just end up with more facts, instead you receive understanding of a heavenly reality. He wants to show you things about who God is, who you are, and what He wants to do in and through your life. He wants you to encounter His kingdom. He wants to teach you truth; He wants to teach you the Scripture!

Look at 1 John 2:27, "As for you, the anointing you received from Him remains in you, and you do not need anyone to teach you. But as his anointing teaches you about all things and as that anointing is real, not counterfeit—just as it has taught you, remain in him" (NIV). The anointing teaches you all things. This does not do away with the need for teachers in the Church, John is emphasizing the need for the ultimate Teacher, the Holy Spirit.

I have had times where I was singing prophetically or praying for someone when I have received revelation from the Holy Spirit. God is bringing revelation through me from His anointing—and I'm being taught by this revelation. When we share revelation, it can be like fresh bread to the soul of the person we are speaking to.

> **God wants to give you His heart and His perspective. He wants to give you His way of seeing things and the way of His kingdom.**

I remember one time I saw a vision of what looked like water pouring from the stage as the worship team was leading. It was like a shallow level of water that was a steady stream flowing. I remembered the vision that Ezekiel had of the water that flowed from the sanctuary in Ezekiel 47. The water was life-giving. I view the deeper levels of water in this chapter of Scripture as symbolizing going deeper in the Spirit.

Jesus talked about "rivers of living water" flowing from within us being the Spirit (John 7:38).

But as I meditated on this vision, the Lord began to show me that the closer you get to the sanctuary, the place of God's Presence, the lower you must go to get in the water. It spoke to me of the humility, reverence, and fear of the Lord that God desires as we draw near to Him.

It is important to note that the Spirit and Word work together. They will never contradict each other. In other words, if the vision or word you are getting isn't lining up with Scripture, you need to reevaluate it. You may need a fresh perspective of the Word, or you may just not be hearing God.

On a more practical note, I make tons of notes in my Bible as I read. I write things that the Lord reveals to me. Those notes become life-giving when I read back through them and receive a fresh heavenly perspective.

There is so much the Lord wants to reveal to us. A prayer I mentioned in an earlier chapter that I pray consistently and encourage you to do the same is from Ephesians 1:17–19, "that the God of our Lord Jesus Christ, the Father of glory, may give to you the spirit of wisdom and revelation in the knowledge of Him, the eyes of your understanding being enlightened."

The bottom line is that God wants to give you His heart and His perspective. He wants to give you His way of seeing things and the way of His kingdom. This insight comes from the Person of the Holy Spirit.

The Holy Spirit Points to Jesus

> But when the Helper comes, whom I shall send to you from the Father, the Spirit of truth who proceeds from the Father, He will testify of Me.
>
> John 15:26

> He will glorify Me, for He will take of what is Mine and declare it to you.
>
> John 16:14

One of the things the Holy Spirit loves to do is point people to Jesus. He is jealous for Jesus to get the glory. He wants to reveal Jesus to you. He wants you to see how glorious, beautiful, and powerful Jesus is.

Remember what Acts 1:8 says, "You will receive power when the Holy Spirit comes on you; and you will be my witnesses" (NIV). The Holy Spirit gives you power to become a witness *for Jesus*. As I mentioned in an earlier chapter, He gives you power to produce supernatural evidence of the reality of Jesus!

> **One of the things the Holy Spirit loves to do is point people to Jesus.**

All throughout the book of Acts, the disciples were demonstrating the power of the Spirit while proclaiming the gospel of Jesus. They knew their mission was to be a witness for Jesus. One of the things we've got to remember when walking in power is that the end goal is to point people to Christ—not ourselves—whether we are speaking to fellow believers or unbelievers.

Jesus is the center of it all. Colossians 1:16–18 says, "For in him all things were created: things in heaven and on earth, visible and invisible, whether thrones or powers or rulers or authorities; all things have been created through him and for him. He is before all things, and in him all things hold together. And he is the head of the body, the church; he is the beginning and the firstborn from among the dead, so that in everything he might have the supremacy" (NIV).

Jesus said that the Holy Spirit would testify of Him and glorify Him. In other words, The Holy Spirit's going to talk about Jesus a lot and make much of Him. Jesus is a big deal to the Holy Spirit.

Symbols of the Holy Spirit

There are a few symbols throughout Scripture that are used to represent the Holy Spirit. It's helpful to recognize these symbols when reading Scripture. This list is meant to assist you in your relationship with the Holy Spirit.

- River/water: Psalm 36:8, 46:4; Ezekiel 47:1–12; John 7:37–39; Revelation 22:1
- Oil: Leviticus 8:12; Psalm 92:10; Isaiah 61:3; 2 Corinthians 1:21–22; Hebrews 1:9
- Breath/wind: Genesis 2:7; Ezekiel 37:9; John 20:22; Acts 2:3
- Rain: Psalm 72:6; Joel 2:23, 28–29
- Wine: Ephesians 5:18
- Dove: Matthew 3:16
- Fire: Matthew 3:11; Acts 2:3

The Holy Spirit Empowers Us

The empowerment of the Holy Spirit is, of course, the topic of this book. Check out what Jesus said in John 16:7, "Nevertheless I tell you the truth. It is to your advantage that I go away; for if I do not go away, the Helper will not come to you; but if I depart, I will send Him to you." I know many of us would love to have Jesus Himself with us in the flesh. But He said that having the Holy Spirit come to live in us is better than having Jesus in the flesh with us. That's a huge statement!

Earlier in John 14:16, Jesus said, "And I will pray the Father, and He will give you another Helper, that He may abide with you forever." The word for "another" is *allos* in the Greek, and it means "another of the same kind."[17] He's saying that when the Helper, the Holy Spirit comes, it will be like having Jesus with you at all times. Dick Mills said Jesus was essentially saying, "He will do in My absence what I would do if I were physically present with you."[18]

The ministry of Jesus continues through the ministry of the Holy Spirit in the saints. To emphasize the focus of this book, Jesus came teaching, preaching, and healing all who were sick. He demonstrated the power of the kingdom of God through miracles, healing, and deliverance. According to Jesus, that ministry is to continue through the Holy Spirit moving through the believers.

Conclusion

The goal of this chapter was to introduce you to the Person of the Holy Spirit. He is a Person you can have relationship with, and He wants to have a friendship with you. As you step into a life of power, make it your goal to be friends with the Holy Spirit.

Activation

WELCOME THE HOLY SPIRIT

Take a few moments to fellowship with the Holy Spirit. Yes, God is omnipresent, He is always everywhere. However, His Presence is not always manifest. We are after the manifest Presence of God.

Here are a few steps you can take to fellowship with the Holy Spirit:

- Open your hands and pray something like this, "Holy Spirit, I welcome You to come. I honor You. You are God. Come and have Your way. I want to know You."
- Take time to worship and sing praise. Psalm 22:3 says that God inhabits our praise. Here are some song suggestions:
    - "Holy Spirit" by Bryan & Katie Torwalt
    - "The Dove" by The Belonging Co.
    - "Ode to the Spirit" by Andrew Hopkins
- Meditate on one of His characteristics from this chapter or one described in Scripture. Then pour out your heart to God in prayer.

You may begin to experience a physical manifestation of His Presence. The Hebrew word for "glory" in the Old Testament is *kavod*,[19] and it's rooted in a word that means "weightiness" or "heaviness."[20] In 2 Chronicles 5:14, as the priests praised the Lord, the Presence of God filled the place so much that "the priests could not perform their service because of the cloud, for the glory of the Lord filled the temple of God" (NIV). They were incapacitated at the glory of God. You might feel that same weight of glory come on you as you minister to the Lord.

You might feel heat. You may tremble at His greatness and because of His power. You may weep and be overwhelmed at His nearness. You may experience peace. You may encounter His love.

The goal is fellowship with the Holy Spirit. Make this a part of your daily relationship with God.

Chapter 4

Speaking in Tongues

> I thank God that I speak in tongues more than all of you.
>
> Apostle Paul, 1 Corinthians 14:18 NIV

I remember ministering in northern Canada at a youth camp a few years ago and there was an unusual flow of the Spirit during the worship time. So, the camp director called the kids forward and we began praying for them. I had the mic and was praying in tongues out loud as I was ministering. There was a guy there who had been a missionary in New Zealand and recognized what I was saying in tongues.

There is a native tribe in New Zealand called the Māori and apparently I was speaking their language.

The young man heard me and said to the lady who runs the camp that I addressed the audience with a personal greeting and the Holy Spirit with a more formal greeting that's generally reserved for very revered figures. I then kept repeating a praise for the Creator, saying He is strong, He leads us, and how powerful the Creator is. The man said he was blown away because I was speaking a full doxology in Māori while preaching about speaking in tongues.

What's crazy is I did an Ancestry DNA test and found out that I have a small percentage of Māori in my DNA. How awesome is God!

God was clearly ministering to this young missionary, but He was also encouraging me and expanding what I thought was possible. It's one thing to read about people supernaturally speaking in unknown languages in Acts 2, but when you experience it yourself, it brings the reality of God in such a powerful way.

The most common evidence in the New Testament that someone was baptized with the Holy Spirit was if the person spoke with tongues. In fact, it was the first thing the disciples in the upper room did after they were filled, "And they were all filled with the Holy Spirit and began to speak with other tongues, as the Spirit gave them utterance" (Acts 2:4). Some people call tongues the initial evidence of the baptism of the Holy Spirit.

> **Here's an important statement: Tongues are for every believer.**

Later, in Acts 10, Peter was preaching at the home of a man named Cornelius and the Bible says, "While Peter was still speaking these words, the Holy Spirit fell upon all those who heard the word...For they heard them speak with tongues and magnify God" (Acts 10:44, 46). Then in Acts 19, Paul runs into some disciples who needed the baptism of the Holy Spirit. "And when Paul had laid hands on them, the Holy Spirit came upon them, and they spoke with tongues and prophesied"

(Acts 19:6). Tongues were the most common manifestation when people got filled with the Holy Spirit.

Here's an important statement: Tongues are for every believer. Jesus said in Mark 16:17, "And these signs will follow those who believe: In My name they will cast out demons; they will speak with new tongues." I'm not saying you *have to* speak in tongues in order to be saved, I'm saying you *get to* speak in tongues! It's available to every believer!

Different Kinds of Tongues

The gift of tongues is when God gives someone the supernatural ability to speak in a language unknown to the speaker for prayer, praise, and prophecy. I want to cover three types of tongues that the Scriptures speak about. Now, it might be funny to use the word "tongues" when what we're really talking about is "languages," but we'll keep it as tongues since most translations of the Bible say tongues.

TONGUES OF MEN

The first time we encounter the gift of tongues in the Bible is in Acts 2. A hundred and twenty disciples were seeking the Lord in the upper room when "suddenly there came a sound from heaven, as of a rushing mighty wind, and it filled the whole house where they were sitting. Then there appeared to them divided tongues, as of fire, and one sat upon each of them. And they were all filled with the Holy Spirit and began to speak with other tongues, as the Spirit gave them utterance" (Acts 2:2–4).

Then the Bible says, "And there were dwelling in Jerusalem Jews, devout men, from every nation under heaven. And when this sound occurred, the multitude came together, and were confused, because *everyone heard them speak in his own language.* Then they were all amazed and marveled, saying to one another, 'Look, are not all these who speak Galileans? And *how is it that we hear, each in our own language in which we were born?* Parthians and Medes and Elamites, those dwelling in Mesopotamia, Judea and Cappadocia, Pontus and Asia, Phrygia and Pamphylia, Egypt and the parts of Libya adjoining Cyrene, visitors from Rome, both Jews and proselytes, Cretans and Arabs—we hear them speaking in our own tongues *the wonderful works of God.*' So they were all amazed and perplexed, saying to one another, 'Whatever could this mean?'" (Acts 2:5–12).

Peter took the opportunity and stood up to preach, "But this is what was spoken by the prophet Joel: 'And it shall come to pass in the last days, says God, That I will pour out of My Spirit on all flesh" (Acts 2:16–17). The result was that 3,000 people gave their lives to Jesus on the day of Pentecost.

> **Tongues build faith, encourage, and communicate God's heart to man.**

Sometimes, when a person speaks in tongues, that person speaks in an earthly language—a language that can be taught and spoken by other people. These are the tongues of men. It's not that Peter and the other disciples went to school and learned the language of the Parthians, Medes, Elamites, etc. Instead, the all-knowing Holy Spirit gifted them the ability to supernaturally speak in the tongues of men. Each gift of the Holy Spirit is supernatural, as Paul makes clear in the following Scripture, "But the *manifestation of the Spirit* is given to each one for the profit of all" (1 Corinthians 12:7).

Remember, the purpose of the baptism of the Spirit is that we would have power to be a witness for Jesus; to produce supernatural evidence of the reality of Jesus. And this power can manifest in God giving us a language of man that we never learned naturally. Tongues reveal the reality of God. Tongues build faith, encourage, and communicate God's heart to man.

The tongues of man still happen today. One time, my church's young adult group was doing a prayer walk on a local university campus. It came to our attention that one of the young men with us hadn't been baptized in the Spirit. So, we prayed for him, and he started speaking Mandarin Chinese! The reason we knew this was because another young man present had lived in China for six years as a missionary with his parents, and he understood what was being said. I believe it served as a faith boost not only for all of us but also the young man who knew Mandarin.

This gift of tongues works on the mission field to draw the lost to Christ, as it did in Acts 2, but it also works to reveal God to those who believe in Christ already.

TONGUES AND INTERPRETATION

I brought my youth leaders to a conference years ago and in the afternoon session the speaker was preaching on the baptism of the Holy Spirit. I came in a bit late, but as he was praying, I went to sit where my youth group was and one of the young girls came up to me and said, "Pastor, I understand what everyone is saying when they're speaking in tongues." I was amazed! She said the speaker, as he was praying in tongues, was praying, "Pour out Your Spirit." God had given this twelve-year-old the gift of interpreting tongues!

Another time, we had a young adult retreat, and I felt from the Spirit that I should bring a friend up to deliver a message in tongues with interpretation. She came up, spoke in tongues, and then interpreted the message. It was wild—she ended up preaching the first section of the sermon I was about to preach that night! This moment was so spot on, and it encouraged me to know I was right on track.

This type of tongue is an unknown tongue, and the Holy Spirit grants the person speaking or hearing it the interpretation of what is being said. It's not the same as the tongues of men, where the hearer understands what is being said because at one time, he or she learned it; it's a supernatural gift of interpretation.

Paul says in 1 Corinthians 14:5–6, "I would like every one of you to speak in tongues, but I would rather have you prophesy. The one who prophesies is greater than the one who speaks in tongues, *unless someone interprets, so that the church may be edified*. Now, brothers and sisters, if I come to you and speak in tongues, what good will I be to you, unless I bring you some *revelation or knowledge or prophecy or word of instruction?*" (NIV)

So, when someone gets up in a congregation and speaks in this kind of tongue, someone should interpret. Not because it's a horrendous sin to not interpret it, but because it's not helpful! If you don't understand the speaker, how could you be encouraged? Paul goes on to say, "Therefore, if I do not know the meaning of the language, I shall be a foreigner to him who speaks, and he who speaks will be a foreigner to me" (1 Corinthians 14:11). However, if there's an interpretation, then the message gets communicated.

The interpretation comes so that the Church can be built up. When that interpretation comes, it gives insight from the Lord that is uplifting to the Church. The one speaking can receive the interpretation or God may give the interpretation to another (1 Corinthians 14:13). The big picture is that God wants to communicate something, and the goal is to build up the Church.

PERSONAL DEVOTIONAL LANGUAGE

> For he who speaks in a tongue does not speak to men but to God, for no one understands him; however, in the spirit he speaks mysteries.
>
> 1 Corinthians 14:2

When I say that tongues are for every believer, I am referring to the tongues of personal devotional language. "And these signs will follow those who believe...they will speak with new tongues" (Mark 16:17). And as we've already seen at in Acts 2, 10, and 19, it wasn't a select few who spoke in tongues when the Holy Spirit came on them, it was all the believers assembled! We don't *have to* speak in tongues, we *get to*! Every believer has the privilege of accessing this devotional prayer language.

> **❝ We don't *have to* speak in tongues, we *get to*!**

This type of tongue is when the Holy Spirit supernaturally gives us a language to pray and praise God with. It's a gift to enhance your relationship with God. I was leading worship a while back and began to sing in tongues. A guy came up to me at the end of the service and told me that I was singing in Latin! He said that I sang, "Glory to You, with the voice of my heart." It was such unique wording of adoration that it surprised me. I wouldn't have chosen that wording, but the Spirit did.

This devotional prayer language can take our intimacy with God to another level. Intimacy with God is a spiritual thing. Remember, Jesus said, "God is Spirit, and those who worship Him must worship in spirit and truth" (John 4:24). Worship and prayer in the Spirit are communing with God on His level—He *is* Spirit.

It's as if the Holy Spirit is taking you into the glory that the Trinity had before the world began (see John 17:5). Where the Son praises the Father, the Father loves the Son, and the Spirit magnifies the Son. Praying in the Spirit is direct communion with God and it's one of the best ways to go deeper in God.

Something unique about the gift of tongues is that you are in control of its usage. In other words, you can turn it on or turn it off. Some people are waiting for a power to take them over and make them speak, but that's not how it works. Look at Acts 2:4 again, "And they were all filled with the Holy Spirit and began to speak with other tongues, as the Spirit gave them utterance." The Spirit gives the words, but *you* are the speaker.

Here are a few benefits of speaking in devotional language tongues:

TONGUES: EDIFY YOU

> He who speaks in a tongue edifies himself
>
> 1 Corinthians 14:4

Edify means to improve or benefit. It comes from a Greek word that means to build a house.[21] You are building yourself up spiritually when you speak in tongues. In the same way prophecy would edify the entire Church—by strengthening, encouraging, and comforting the body of believers—tongues do the same for the individual.

Regarding tongues as a way of "building a house," Mahesh Chavda said, "I would ask every believer: Is your structure a skyscraper or a shack? If you feel your structure is small, there is a God-given plan for how you can build yourself up and add on to your faith."[22] Jude 20 says, "But you, beloved, building yourselves up on your most holy faith, praying in the Holy Spirit."

Connecting with God is edifying. If you're communing with God by the Spirit, your life will be benefited. Galatians 6:8 says it like this, "he who sows to the Spirit will of the Spirit reap everlasting life." Jesus said that eternal life is knowing God (John 17:3). One of the ways we sow to the Spirit is by praying in tongues.

Paul said in 1 Corinthians 14:28, "But if there is no interpreter, let him keep silent in church, and *let him speak to himself and to God.*" It's interesting to me that it doesn't just say "to God" but also "to himself." Going back to the testimony of the young man supernaturally speaking in Mandarin Chinese, our friend who had lived in China told us what he was saying. He said the guy kept repeating, "You believe in Him, you believe in Him!" We had a literal manifestation of him speaking "to himself" in tongues! It was like the Lord was commanding him to have faith as he was speaking in tongues.

The different types of tongues can overlap and work together. For example, the young man speaking in Mandarin (i.e., the tongues of men) was also edifying himself. Similarly, a friend of mine from the missions movement, YWAM, shared with me that as he was praying in a prayer room in China, a Chinese man began to pray in Spanish. This man was praying in an unknown tongue, but his tongue could be understood by someone who did speak Spanish. God supernaturally enabled him to speak in Spanish as part of his intercession. My friend, being from Southern California, knew this man was praying in Spanish. After conversation, my friend learned that the Chinese man did not know Spanish but was speaking Spanish by the Spirit. The gift of tongues is multifaceted and often the Spirit will use different types of tongues together.

I believe one of the reasons we receive edification when praying in tongues is that we are declaring the word of the Lord over ourselves, as led by the Spirit. As a side note, some people don't like repetition in worship or even prayer, but we often need to hear truth repeatedly. This is part of how meditation works!

I believe praying in tongues activates the *dunamis* power of the Holy Spirit in our lives. It's like we're plugging ourselves into a power source and getting charged up. Just as our smartphones do not last long without a charge, our spiritual lives need to be plugged into the source, that is, our God. One of the ways we stay charged up with *dunamis* power is to pray in tongues.

When you are edified, built up, and charged with the power of the Spirit, you become a powerful vessel used to go and edify others.

TONGUES: PERFECT PRAYER

I pray in tongues more than I pray in English. The Holy Spirit knows what I need to pray for way more than I do. Think about it, if the Spirit is giving the utterance, then those prayers are exactly what we need to be praying. Instead of shooting arrows into the dark, when we pray in tongues, we are hitting the target every time. We are praying perfect prayers!

We don't always know what to pray for, but the Holy Spirit does. He could lead us in intercession for a family member, lead us to pray for our job, or lead us to praise God and declare His wonderful works. Whatever we need, the Holy Spirit knows.

I believe that God can give us understanding of what we're saying when we're praying in tongues. First Corinthians 14:13 says, "Therefore let him who speaks in a tongue pray that he may interpret." Yes, the immediate application of this verse is for the public use of tongues, but I also believe we can interpret our own prayer language to God.

Here's how this works in my own life. As I said in the last chapter, I'll be praying in the Spirit and things "come up on my screen," just like a notification on my smartphone. It could be anything from a Scripture the Lord is highlighting, a prophetic word, a song I should lead that week to a topic I should preach, a reminder to connect with my wife or kids, or a small task to do around the house or for the ministry. God is involved in all areas of our lives.

The Holy Spirit truly is our helper.

TONGUES: KEEP YOU SPIRITUALLY MINDED

> For if I pray in a tongue, my spirit prays, but my mind is unfruitful. So what shall I do? I will pray with my spirit, but I will also pray with my understanding; I will sing with my spirit, but I will also sing with my understanding.
>
> 1 Corinthians 14:14–15 NIV

One of the things we need to remember is that we're spiritual people first. The gift of tongues is so helpful because it causes us to lean *not* on our own understanding but on the Holy Spirit (see Proverbs 3:5). When we pray in tongues, we don't know what we're saying, and that might scare us. This gift will help us dethrone our fleshly minds and think from the Spirit, from the mind of Christ.

It doesn't make sense to the natural mind that we lay hands on the sick and they recover. It doesn't make sense to the natural mind that we could prophesy the secrets of someone's heart without knowing them beforehand. It doesn't make sense to the natural mind that we could communicate a message in a language we've never learned before. But to the spiritually minded person, these things *do* make sense.

Look at what Paul said in Romans 8:6, "The mind governed by the flesh is death, but the mind governed by the Spirit is life and peace" (NIV). Your flesh doesn't want anything to do with God. It will fight against you when you want to worship, pray, or seek God. It will fight against you when you want to read the Scriptures, go to church, or minister to someone. Jesus said it like this, "The spirit indeed is willing, but the flesh is weak." (Matthew 26:41). You've got to strengthen yourself in the Spirit!

Your born-again spirit, your new creation nature wants to seek God, wants to know Him, wants to worship and pray, wants to minister, and wants to hear from God. When you pray in the Spirit, you are prioritizing your spiritual nature. You are learning to live from your spirit instead of your flesh. You're connecting to the heart of God and living from that place. Praying in tongues is one of the best ways to get us out of our own fleshly minds and into the Spirit—out of our own way of thinking and into the mind of Christ.

I encourage every believer to use this personal devotional language of tongues every day. Paul said, "I thank my God that I speak in tongues more than all of you; yet in the church I would rather speak five words with my understanding, that I may teach others also, than ten thousand words in a tongue" (1 Corinthians 14:18–19).

The church of Corinth was the most charismatic church of their day. Paul had to write them a letter to correct their out of hand usage of the gifts of the Spirit. Suffice it to say, that this church spoke in tongues *a lot*. But Paul said he spoke in tongues more than them all! Since he wasn't speaking in tongues at their church, his personal devotional life must have been *overflowing* with prayer and praise in tongues!

I encourage believers today to do the same.

Answering Common Questions

CAN EVERY BELIEVER SPEAK IN TONGUES?

Yes! If you're a believer in Jesus Christ, you are qualified to speak in tongues. I have noticed sometimes people assume the following verse prohibits them from speaking in tongues,

> Are all apostles? Are all prophets? Are all teachers? Are all workers of miracles? Do all have gifts of healings? Do all speak with tongues? Do all interpret?
>
> 1 Corinthians 12:29–30

Obviously, Paul makes it clear that not every believer speaks in tongues. But when we compare this passage with what Jesus said in Mark 16:17, "And these signs will follow those who believe: In My name they will cast out demons; they will speak with new tongues," and the context of Acts 2, 10, and 19, where the *entire group* of believers present spoke in tongues, we see the bigger picture.

When we look at the context of 1 Corinthians 12, we see that the things Paul is naming are ministries. For example, not everyone will have the ministry of an apostle, a prophet, or a worker of miracles. Not everyone will have the ministry of tongues or interpretation. This is why we need the body of Christ. Everyone plays a significant role.

Then what was Jesus referring to? How come every believer present in Acts 2, 10, and 19 all spoke with tongues? I believe these verses are pointing to the fact that, while not everyone will have the *ministry* of tongues and interpretation, we all have access to the *personal devotional language* of tongues.

> **While not everyone will have the *ministry* of tongues and interpretation, we all have access to the *personal devotional language* of tongues.**

I will say, however, if God wants to, He can use you to deliver a message in tongues or interpret a message, even though that may not be your main gift. I wouldn't say of myself that I have the gift of tongues as a ministry, but I have been used to deliver a message in tongues.

Paul said in 1 Corinthians 12:31, "But earnestly desire the best gifts." The word for "best" means more useful, more serviceable, more advantageous.[23] Paul is saying to desire the gift that works best for the moment. Earlier in 1 Corinthians 12:11 Paul said that the Spirit will distribute the gifts as He wills. Somewhere in between our seeking and His will, the best gift for the occasion comes forth.

So, if God sees it fit to deliver a message in tongues, but that's not your main gift, you might still be called upon by the Lord to release the word! While it may not be your ministry, don't exclude yourself from the gift.

ARE WE ALLOWED TO SPEAK/SING IN TONGUES IN PUBLIC SETTINGS?

Yes! However, it all depends on the context. In the book of Acts, particularly in chapters 2, 10, and 19, you have groups of believers gathered together, all speaking in tongues, no one is interpreting, and everything is good. In 1 Corinthians 14, however, Paul instructs the church to make sure they have an interpreter if someone is speaking in tongues at their gatherings. If not, the person speaking in tongues was to remain silent.

So, according to Scripture, there are times when it's appropriate and times when it's not. Sometimes you need an interpreter, sometimes you don't.

If you're in a gathering where informed believers are present, I don't see anything wrong with everyone lifting their voice in their devotional language, whether in prayer or praise. Do I still think someone should say something in a known language? Yes, of course, people need to be corporately edified! But if you know there are uninformed or unbelievers around, use discretion with your devotional language and employ an interpreter if there is a tongue for interpretation. In fact, in any meeting, if anyone has a tongue that needs interpretation, someone should give the interpretation. I would like to add, however, that you won't see the various ways tongues can be used in a corporate setting unless you employ them.

Paul closes 1 Corinthians 14 with these words, "Therefore, brethren, desire earnestly to prophesy, and do not forbid to speak with tongues. Let all things be done decently and in order" (39–40). We have to let things be done before they can be put in order. Some churches, because of fear of things getting indecent and out of order, don't let the spiritual gifts flow. None of the testimonies I shared in this chapter would have happened if people only spoke in tongues in private. The various church cultures I was in gave freedom to flow in the gift of tongues and some amazing God-moments happened as a result.

In Conclusion

Let's recap:

- All believers have access to the personal devotional language of tongues.
- God may use you in the tongues of men or tongues and interpretation, be open!
- Pray daily in devotional tongues!

Activation

RECEIVE YOUR PRAYER LANGUAGE

If you haven't yet received the baptism of the Holy Spirit, go back to the activation at the end of Chapter 2 and use that as a guide. Many times, people will receive the gift of tongues when they are baptized in the Holy Spirit.

If you've received the baptism of the Spirit, but haven't received the gift of tongues yet, here are some Scriptures to guide you as you seek the gift of tongues.

ASK!

> So I say to you, ask, and it will be given to you; seek, and you will find; knock, and it will be opened to you.
>
> Luke 11:9

BE OPEN!

> "If a son asks for bread from any father among you, will he give him a stone? Or if he asks for a fish, will he give him a serpent instead of a fish? Or if he asks for an egg, will he offer him a scorpion?"
>
> Luke 11:11

RECEIVE AND SPEAK!

> All of them were filled with the Holy Spirit and began to speak in other tongues, as the Spirit enabled them.
>
> Acts 2:4 NIV

You may want to have someone who flows in the gift of tongues lay hands on you and pray with you.

Here is a prayer you can pray if you would like to receive the gift of tongues:

"Father, fill me afresh with the Holy Spirit. I ask You to give me the gift of tongues. I believe You give good gifts, and this prayer language is one of those gifts. Right now, I receive this gift by faith, in Jesus' name!"

Once you've prayed, it's time to speak! Whatever the Lord gives, just speak it out. It may sound like gibberish. It may not make sense to your mind. Some people think they're just making it up, but this is where faith kicks in.

Thank God for His gift!

Now pray in this language every day and expect its benefits to manifest in your life.

Chapter 5

Prophesy!

> And it shall come to pass in the last days, says God, that I will pour out of My Spirit on all flesh; Your sons and your daughters shall prophesy.
>
> Acts 2:17, Apostle Peter quoting Joel 2:28

One of the main results of the outpouring of the Spirit at Pentecost was that we would become a prophetic people! This wasn't for the "super-spiritual" or those who studied years and years at a high-level university. The prophetic was meant for sons and daughters! The prophet Joel and the apostle Peter made it clear: We were meant to be a prophetic people.

What does that mean? Prophecy is simply God speaking through us. Prophetic people hear God and speak what He says. Prophetic people carry the heart of the Father and release it to others. Sometimes prophecy foretells what will happen and many times it's forthtelling, speaking forth a message on God's heart. As a son or daughter of God, God wants to prophesy through you!

I remember in 2018, I received four prophetic words about recording an album. A man of God came to a meeting I was leading worship in, took off his watch, and as a prophetic sign, gave it to me saying, "The Lord says, now is the time to record your album." I received the word and the watch and was grateful. But you know what I did? Nothing.

Not too long after, a friend of mine was doing a prophetic exercise for a class she was taking, and sent me a word with the same phrase, "Now is the time!" Another friend had a dream with me in it and said she came up to me in the dream and heard a song that said, "Now is the time!"

If I had any doubts that God was speaking, the confirmations were coming.

I received even more confirmation. I was ministering in Big Bear, California, and the man of God who hosted the meetings asked me if I was recording my music. Then he said, "Well, I just feel like the Lord is saying now is the time." Clearly, it was time to record the album!

I finally started making plans with my producer, put a budget together, and started to raise money. I had received another word from a prophet saying, "Andrew, I see you in the studio recording an album, and God says He is going to provide for it!" That was good to hear since the budget was around $21,000 and my bank account—well, had not received the fulfilled prophecy yet.

So, what did I do? I took those prophetic words to prayer and said, "God, You said it's time to record this album and that You would provide. So let it come forth in Jesus' name." And within five weeks, all the money I needed came in and the project was finished that year! These words and provision brought about my album, *Send Out Your Roar*.

God had it in His heart that I would record and release an album that year, so He sent His sons and daughters to prophesy to me. The prophetic words came to me to give direction and faith for provision. Prophetic words do a host of things. They can encourage, strengthen, comfort, and guide us. Many times, prophetic words come as confirmations of what God has already been speaking to us. Prophecy shares what is on the heart of the Father.

> But the one who prophesies speaks to people for their strengthening, encouraging and comfort.
>
> 1 Corinthians 14:3 NIV

> How precious are your thoughts about me, O God. They cannot be numbered!
>
> I can't even count them; they outnumber the grains of sand!
>
> Psalm 139:17–18 NLT

God wants to strengthen, encourage, comfort, direct, give gifts, give faith, give clarity, set free, and bless people through prophecy! He has no shortage of things to say. His thoughts outnumber the grains of sand.

Can you imagine an army of people who carry the heart of the Father and release it wherever they go? People need to know God sees them, that God cares about them. We need to tell people that God sees what they've gone through, God has plans for their futures and so much more. One of the best ways to demonstrate God's love for people is when sons and daughters prophesy!

> Let love be your highest goal! But you should also desire the special abilities the Spirit gives—especially the ability to prophesy.
>
> 1 Corinthians 14:1 NLT

Ways to Hear God

The first part of prophecy is hearing God. You were created to hear God. We were made to have relationship with Him, and relationships involve communication. Prayer is talking to God; prophecy is God talking to us.

> **The outpouring of the Spirit makes you a prophetic person.**

Jesus said it like this, "My sheep hear My voice, and I know them, and they follow Me." (John 10:27). And the Scripture says that when you receive the outpouring of the Spirit, you will prophesy. In other words, you will hear God and speak what He's speaking. The outpouring of the Spirit makes you a prophetic person.

So, how do you hear God? Here are three foundational ways we can hear God speaking.

HEAR

This might sound obvious and I don't want to be redundant, but you hear God through *hearing*. Remember, Jesus said, "My sheep *hear* My voice" (John 10:27). There is the possibility of hearing God's audible voice. This happened many times in Scripture, like when the Father spoke over Jesus at His baptism saying, "This is My beloved Son, in whom I am well pleased." (Matthew 3:17). However, I would say this is not the most common way of hearing God.

Most people often hear God through His "still small voice." This phrase comes from the story of Elijah the prophet not hearing God speak in a loud and flashy way, but rather he heard God in a still small voice (1 Kings 19:11–13). Just because you don't hear a strong, booming voice that sounds like Mufasa from *The Lion King*, it doesn't mean it's not God. God's voice can come in a whisper but still carry the power of the thunder. You don't just *hear* the thunder; you *feel* the thunder. That's how it is when God speaks—you hear it, but you also feel it. There's a substance to His words—the substance of His Spirit.

> At this also my heart trembles, and leaps from its place. Hear attentively the thunder of His voice, and the rumbling that comes from His mouth.
>
> Job 37:1–2

> "It is the Spirit who gives life; the flesh profits nothing. The words that I speak to you are spirit, and they are life."
>
> John 6:63

I often hear the still small voice of God on the inside. Sometimes I'll hear a Scripture verse, a phrase, or a word. Sometimes, I'll get some tasks to do, and other times God will speak to me about how He feels about me. But, when I'm prophesying, I'm hearing God for other people. So, I'll share what I hear—a Scripture, word, or message—and encourage them with that.

There have been times when I, as a worship leader, will start singing the Scriptures off the pastor's notes that I've never seen, or as I'm praying for people God reveals things about their lives that I didn't know. Other times I'm calling forth destiny and prophesying things to come and what God is going to do in people's lives.

One time I was leading worship and we entered into a throne room kind of moment. I quoted Isaiah 6:8, "Then I heard the voice of the Lord saying, 'Whom shall I send? And who will go for us?' And I said, 'Here am I. Send me!'" and then I prophesied that God was calling people to the nations (NIV). What I didn't know was there was a guy at the meeting that God was telling to return to Uganda. When I prophesied from Isaiah 6:8, he started weeping and knew God was confirming his call to Uganda.

God wants to activate your ears to hear.

> "He who has an ear, let him hear what the Spirit says to the churches."
>
> Revelation 3:22

SEE

> I will look to see what he will say to me.
>
> Habakkuk 2:1 NIV

One of the Old Testament words for prophets is "seers." You guessed it, because they saw in the realm of the Spirit. The next part of the opening verse in this chapter says, "Your young men shall see visions" (Acts 2:17). The verse is not limiting who can see. Young men are not the only ones who can see visions, and prophecy is for sons and daughters! The Scripture gives us another way that the prophetic operates: seeing.

In Isaiah 6, the prophet Isaiah saw the throne room. He saw the Lord on the throne, the angels flying around and worshipping, and the train of the Lord's robe filled the temple. In Ezekiel 37, the prophet Ezekiel saw the valley of dry bones come to life. These men were seeing in another dimension. In the Psalms, David prophesied of the coming Messiah and described what would happen (see Psalm 2 and 22). He was seeing prophetically.

Prophetic sight is what I function in most often. Frequently, I'll see a picture, a vision, or a Scripture, and God will speak to me about its meaning. When you see things from the Lord, ask Him what they mean. There's an old saying that goes, "A picture is worth a thousand words." That picture you see could communicate many different things, but you want to know what God wants to say through it.

> **God wants to open your spiritual eyes to see.**

One time I was playing music at a coffee shop. I wrote a song a while back on healing, and as I was singing it, I saw a picture of a foot with a red, throbbing look on the heel; much like you'd see in a commercial for pain reliever. I figured it was a word for healing. At the end of the song, I shared what I saw and commanded the heel to be healed. Then I moved on.

My mom was at the coffee shop, and after I was done with my set, I walked her back to her car. She asked me, "How did you know about that heel thing?" I explained to her what I saw and what a word of knowledge was and she told me, "That's weird, because I came here with pain in my heel and now it's not there anymore!"

Now, technically this situation involved a word of knowledge gift working with the gift of healing, but I'm sharing it because it started with something I saw.

I wrote another book called *Fierce Peace* based on a vision and encounter I had with the Prince of Peace. I saw a man standing across from me, clothed in armor, holding out a sword. The encounter ended with me laying and resting on my back while Jesus stood guard over me with His sword drawn. I realized I had just experienced Philippians 4:7

which says that the peace of God "will guard your hearts and minds through Christ Jesus" and this became a message that I carry.

God wants to open your spiritual eyes to see. This is shown in the prayer I have mentioned multiple times now in this book from Ephesians,

> I pray that the Father of glory, the God of our Lord Jesus Christ, would impart to you the riches of the Spirit of wisdom and the Spirit of revelation to know him through your deepening intimacy with him. I pray that the light of God will illuminate the eyes of your imagination, flooding you with light.
>
> Ephesians 1:17–18 TPT

SPEAK

The Hebrew word for prophecy means, "to cause to bubble up, hence, to pour forth words abundantly."[24] Prophecy happens when God's words start to "bubble up" from within you and you start speaking. I use the analogy of a tissue box to express this. You have that one tissue sticking out of the top, and when you grab that one, another one comes up. God may give you a word to speak and as you release that one, another word comes up, and so on.

> Then the Lord put forth His hand and touched my mouth, and the Lord said to me: "Behold, I have put My words in your mouth."
>
> Jeremiah 1:9

I've noticed this happens when I begin to pray for people. I may start praying a generic blessing, but then suddenly, the anointing comes on me and I start prophesying. The faith I used to step out and pray activated the prophetic and then the words began bubbling up. I've found that when I create opportunities that put a demand on the prophetic, the prophetic starts flowing.

Paul said to "eagerly desire gifts of the Spirit, especially prophecy" (1 Corinthians 14:1 NIV).

We saw this happen at a local university campus when a group from my church would go and minister. We would start conversations with people and from there the Lord would give us words to share with people.

God wants to put His words in your mouth!

> Open wide your mouth, and I will fill it.
>
> Psalm 81:10 NIV

It all comes down to your personal relationship with the Holy Spirit. Yes, there is a supernatural gift that can come on you, but I've found that the more I grow in my friendship with God, the easier it is for me to hear Him.

The more your relationship with God grows, you'll learn to recognize Him and learn how He speaks to you. God can also speak to you through:

- Dreams
- A sense of knowing
- Nature
- Signs and wonders
- Songs
- Objects
- Names

Remember: Prophecy isn't sharing our words; it's sharing God's words!

Interpret the Word

I encourage you that once you've received something from the Lord, ask Him what it means.

If He gives you a Scripture verse for someone, ask Him what He wants to say through it. If He gives you a picture, ask Him what He is saying through it. Maybe He'll give you a character from history—ask Him what it is about that person that He wants to communicate to others.

The best way to interpret the meaning of a word you receive is through the Scriptures. The Scriptures hold keys to understanding. A lot of times, I will see an image or a picture of something and I run it through Scripture to find the meaning.

For example, when my wife and I were praying for a family recently, I saw a bunch of warrior-type angels behind them. I was reminded of the story of Elisha and his servant in 2 Kings 6:15–17 where the Syrian army had surrounded Elisha, but he saw in the realm of the Spirit that the mountain was full of horses and chariots of fire. God was for them even though an army was against them. The word I prophesied to the family, amongst many other things, was "There are more for you than those who are against you."

If I see a hammer in a vision, I can go to Jeremiah 23:29, "'Is not My word like a fire?' says the Lord, 'And like a hammer that breaks the rock in pieces?'" In such a case, perhaps the Lord wants to speak about breakthrough in someone's life.

If I see a broom, I can go to Luke 15:8–10 where a woman lost a silver coin and swept the whole house looking for it. One interpretation of the broom could be that God is reaching out towards someone that is lost.

Of course, these are just a few examples. The Scriptures are a key to understanding what you see prophetically. Not only in the literal sense of seeing something that is in Scripture but also in the heart of God revealed in the Word. Don't try to reveal God's heart through prophecy if you haven't taken in His heart already revealed in the Scriptures!

Filters for Your Words

When you receive what you feel are words from the Lord, you want to have a filtering system to run them through. The reality is, that God still speaks, but our understanding is not always perfect. In prophetic ministry, these filters help to make sure we're in line with the heart of God.

IS THE PROPHETIC WORD SCRIPTURAL?

Scripture is the ultimate authority on what we're hearing. If it doesn't line up with the Bible, then we should throw it out! This, of course, requires that we know the Word. We've got to spend enough time in the Word to catch the heart of God and know what the Scriptures teach. We need to take time to study the Word and get a Biblical framework for life and ministry. The Bible reveals the heart and mind of God.

> **Scripture is the ultimate authority on what we're hearing.**

It goes without saying, but modern-day prophecy is not creating more Scriptures. The Bible is a closed book and will not be added to. We're functioning in the gift of prophecy the way the New Testament churches did and were instructed to. For example, the church in Corinth had all kinds of prophecy going on, but we don't know what was prophesied because it didn't make it in the Bible! In other words, it wasn't Scripture-level prophecy that should have been recorded for generations to come and guide the doctrines of the church. People were simply hearing from God and sharing what they heard on a personal level.

When you get words for people, make sure they're biblical!

IS THE PROPHETIC WORD HELPFUL?

> But the one who prophesies speaks to people for their strengthening, encouraging and comfort...the one who prophesies edifies the church.
>
> 1 Corinthians 14:3–4 NIV

Is your word strengthening, encouraging, or comforting? Does it build someone up?

More seasoned prophets have a call to bring prophetic correction and even direction, but that isn't what most people are called to do. In hearing God for others, we want to make it our goal to lift people up, call them higher, and have them walking away with more courage in their hearts to go after God and what He's called them to do.

If you receive a word that reveals something negative about a person, instead of telling them what's wrong with them, speak in the opposite spirit. Call them out of their darkness and into the light. Prophecy is encouraging, not discouraging.

That's what Ezekiel did in the valley of dry bones. He saw a valley full of bones. But when the word of the Lord came to him, he prophesied life (see Ezekiel 37). He didn't prophesy, "Thus says the Lord, you are DEAD and DRY!" He prophesied life and the bones came together, skin came on them, and an army came alive!

God is the God who "calls those things which do not exist as though they did" (Romans 4:17).

Remember the cross of Christ changes everything. The Scripture says "that God was reconciling the world to himself in Christ, not counting people's sins against them. And he has committed to us the message of reconciliation" (2 Corinthians 5:19 NIV). Let your prophetic ministry be filtered through the finished work of Jesus' cross!

IS THE PROPHETIC WORD OUT OF BOUNDS?

Here's a general rule when prophesying—no dates, mates, or babies.

When you're learning to prophesy, steer clear of these subjects in your words. Even seasoned prophets rarely step into these waters. You may hear things related to those topics, but I recommend keeping those things between you and the Lord and letting them play out. If you ended up hearing correctly, praise God. If not, you can learn from the situation.

Let me just say it clearly: Do not prophesy to a member of the opposite sex that you two are supposed to get married! Don't match-make with anyone. Prophetic ministry should not be manipulative. Do not prophesy if or when people are going to have babies and do not tell them, "By this date, this thing will happen."

While I would generally encourage risk-taking when it comes to the supernatural, these areas are weightier and if not handled right could cause unnecessary damage.

Paul said in Romans 12:6, "Having then gifts differing according to the grace that is given to us, let us use them: if prophecy, let us prophesy in proportion to our faith." In other words, don't go beyond your measure of faith and authority.

This means at least two things to me. One, recognize spiritual authority and your position in the body of Christ. Don't take a higher position of authority than what has been given to you. Two, don't overreach in your prophetic words. It is unlikely that God will use a novice believer to prophesy the next pastor of the church or bring a word for the nation.

I don't say this to discourage but to give healthy boundaries to function within.

How to Prophesy

Hear from God, ask Him what the words or vision you are given mean, run it through the filters, and speak!

Here are a few tips when prophesying:

BE POSITIVE

We've covered this already, but it's worth mentioning again. Follow the way of love! Read 1 Corinthians 13 for a refresher. Paul said that if we could prophesy and know all mysteries but don't have love, we are nothing. Love is vital.

Let your prophetic words be uplifting.

BE KIND

Kindness is a fruit of the Spirit. When you're communicating with people, show kindness. You have a chance to reveal the heart of the Father!

BE BRIEF

We should try to avoid prophesying for a long time. We're not writing another book of Isaiah. Say what the Lord is saying and then say amen. Some prophetic words are longer than others but stay in the flow of the anointing.

BE HUMBLE

Come as a servant of the Lord. Serve people the word of the Lord.

BE YOURSELF

Don't feel the need to change your accent or unnecessarily shout at someone when prophesying. Be normal, be you!

KNOW THAT YOU DON'T KNOW IT ALL

> For we know in part and we prophesy in part.
>
> 1 Corinthians 13:9

HONOR AUTHORITY

Respect the places you are in and respect the authorities that are established there.

USE A BREATH MINT

Don't distract the person you are prophesying to with bad breath. The phrase, "say it, don't spray it," also applies here. People will thank you later.

ASK FOR FEEDBACK

Ask the person you are prophesying to if the word you delivered makes sense to them. Get feedback on what you prophesied. This can happen right after you prophesy or later when something comes to pass. Learn from the feedback you receive and be encouraged by it.

Start where you're at. Pray for people at church or your small group. Minister to those in the drive-thru or gas station. Share prophetic words with your neighbors.

If I'm prophesying to a person I do not know and we are out in public, I start by saying something like, "Hey, I'm a Christian and sometimes God shares things with me for other people. He shared some stuff with me that I believe is for you. Do you mind if I tell you what I heard?"

If I'm at church, I might approach a person saying, "Hey, can I pray for you?" or "I feel like the Lord is saying this to you."

Testing Words

Let me insert a quick guide for testing prophetic words. This falls more on the side of receiving prophetic words rather than giving them. Nevertheless, it's important to share.

> Do not quench the Spirit. Do not despise prophecies. Test all things; hold fast what is good.
>
> 1 Thessalonians 5:19–21

> Let two or three prophets speak, and let the others judge.
>
> 1 Corinthians 14:29

The Scripture encourages us to test the words we receive. The fact that we should test the words factors in the possibility that we could get it wrong. This doesn't mean someone is a false prophet, it just means they got the word wrong. It's an opportunity to learn.

Sam Storms said, "False prophets are indeed spoken of in the New Testament, but they were not Christians who made errors in prophetic words. False prophets were non-Christian enemies of the gospel."[25] They were those who drew people away from Christ.

It's important to test the words! We want to "chew the meat and spit out the bones." If someone gets a word wrong, they should get corrected and trained! When people get prophetic words right, it changes lives and draws people to Jesus.

FOUR WAYS TO TEST A WORD:

- Scripture
- Bears witness with you
- Bears witness with your leaders
- Bears witness with your community

Words of Knowledge

> For to one is given the word of wisdom through the Spirit, to another the word of knowledge through the same Spirit.
>
> 1 Corinthians 12:8

Another gift I want to highlight in this chapter is the word of knowledge. While prophecy is usually spoken in the present and future tenses, words of knowledge generally speak in the past or present tense. Words of knowledge reveal a piece of information about someone or something. I find that words of knowledge usually work together with the gifts of prophecy or healing.

I remember prophesying to a girl one time and hearing the song "A Whole New World" in my mind. She blurted out, "That's my favorite song!" It was a word of knowledge and a launching point to a prophetic word about a new season in her life. There have been many times the Lord would highlight a body part that needed healing—like the heel I mentioned earlier—and after prayer, the person would be healed.

The word of knowledge revealed a piece of information about each person. In one case it was a launching point for a prophetic word, in the other case it was the access point for healing. One of the functions of words of knowledge is to release faith. When you know God sees you in your situation through a word of knowledge, it boosts your faith to believe He can bring the breakthrough that you need.

Words of knowledge show people that God sees, knows, and loves them. It's like when Jesus ministered to the woman at the well in John 4. He told her of her past and she went back to her town and declared, "Come, see a Man who told me all things that I ever did. Could this be the Christ?" (John 4:29). I remember different times doing campus ministry for college students and people being blown away that I knew things going on in their lives. But it wasn't me, it was God! These were opportunities for them to experience that God was real.

> **Words of knowledge show people that God sees, knows, and loves them.**

In prophetic ministry, words of knowledge are likely to flow alongside your prophecies. They come like prophecies, such as through hearing and seeing. The difference between prophecies and words of knowledge is that words of knowledge are facts about the person's life and prophecy is when God is sharing His heart with them. Words of knowledge come from God's knowledge of everyone and everything. Prophecy comes from God's heart and will for the world.

The goal of both gifts is that Jesus would be revealed to people, and they would experience the love of God.

Permission Granted

In Numbers 11, there's a story of how God took from the Spirit that was on Moses and put it on seventy of the elders. When the Spirit came on them, they started prophesying. There were a couple of men that did not make it to the meeting place, Eldad and Medad. However, they still got the impartation and prophesied where they were!

Joshua found out and told Moses that they needed to stop. Moses replied, "Are you zealous for my sake? Oh, that all the Lord's people were prophets and that the Lord would put His Spirit upon them!" (Numbers 11:29).

In this statement, Moses revealed the heart of God. Joel prophesied later and Peter quoted him: that God would pour out His Spirit on all flesh and sons and daughters would prophesy (Joel 2:28; Acts 2:17). These verses do not mean that everyone will have the title of "prophet," but that all of God's people would be prophetic people. Moses was happy that, at least for that moment, he wasn't the only one prophesying! God's dream is that His people would prophesy.

One time, I prophesied to a young lady that God was going to use her to prophesy. It was a simple word. Now, we were in revival meetings, so we were saturated in a prophetic atmosphere. Yet, up until this point, I don't think she had ever prophesied. A week after the word I gave her, she came back to me saying the word had already come to pass and that she had stepped out and prophesied to a couple of people.

In my mind, I was thinking, *It's about time! She was saturated in a prophetic environment. Who can help but prophesy?* But then I realized she needed permission. She needed the word to call her higher. She needed to be activated. Don't we all need a nudge from the Lord at times? That prophetic word was a bridge for her to cross over into prophetic ministry.

That word was not just for her! I'm prophesying to you now. God is going to use you to prophesy. Now is the time!

Permission granted! Go ahead and prophesy!

Activations

Here is a prayer to ask God to activate you prophetically,

> "Lord, I desire to prophesy. I ask You for the gift of prophecy to be activated in me. I ask You for a fresh outpouring of the Holy Spirit. I receive it now and I thank You for it, in Jesus' name."

Now just take a few moments, hands open, and receive from the Lord. Pray in tongues and wait in His Presence. You may want to turn on a worship song and sing to the Lord. God's Presence comes in praise.

You may want to ask someone who flows in this gift to lay hands on you and pray a prayer of impartation.

Here are a few exercises to activate the prophetic in your life:

HEAR FOR YOURSELF

Close your eyes, open your hands, and ask the Lord, "Jesus, how do you feel about me?" Write down what He says about you.

HEAR FOR SOMEONE ELSE

Close your eyes, open your hands, and ask the Lord, "Jesus, is there anyone you'd like me to give a word to?" Then ask, "Jesus, what message do you want me to share with them?" Then share it with them via text, phone call, email, or in person and ask for their feedback.

GO PUBLIC

As you go throughout your day, look for someone the Lord may highlight to you. God could highlight anyone to you: a coworker, fellow student, server at a restaurant, or a gas station attendant. Ask the Lord for a word for that individual. Deliver the word and, again, make sure to ask for feedback.

Chapter 6

Healing Ministry

> And these signs will follow those who believe…
> they will lay hands on the sick, and they will
> recover.
>
> The Lord Jesus, Mark 16:17–18

God wants to use you to heal the sick. One of the ways that the power of God moves through our lives is in supernatural healing. I'm not talking about emotional, medical, or inner healing—although those types of healings are great and ways God does bring healing. I'm talking about healing miracles that remove the pains, ailments, and diseases in people's physical bodies.

Healing was normal to Jesus' ministry and normal to the disciples' ministry. I submit to you that healing should be normal in your ministry. Healing is still happening today and it's one of the ways God wants to reveal Himself to the world around us. Remember, the power is for a purpose, and the purpose is to point people to Jesus. We are witnesses—people who produce evidence. When the Holy Spirit reveals Jesus through healing miracles, I'd say that's some pretty good evidence.

One time I was preaching at my church's young adult group on the need for power. My message then was similar to the content of this book. In the months leading up to this night, I had seen a bunch of healings in my travels. I saw deafness healed, various pains leaving people's bodies, and a tremor stop in a man's arm. I was excited and had a fresh passion from these testimonies.

At the end of the service, I prayed for people and hung around. A girl came up to me and began to ask about the power of God. She said that for years of her life, she had to wear a brace on her knee—which she happened to leave at home that night—because her patella was slipping, and she would deal with severe pain. I prayed for her, and the power of God touched her knee and she testified later that she felt tissue growing around the kneecap. She didn't need her brace anymore!

The healing was powerful, but she shared later that that one miracle had shifted her entire life. She encountered the Person of the Holy Spirit and began pursuing Him passionately. God set her free from self-harm and depression and began to cause reconciliation in her family. Praise God!

> **God has called every believer into healing ministry.**

I share this girl's story to show you the impact that the power of God can have on people's lives. It's not just for the apostles of old, people with healing ministries, or a guy with a microphone—the ability to bring healing is for the everyday believer. God has called every believer into healing ministry (Mark 16:18).

God's Will to Heal

The first thing you need to know is that God *wants* to heal people! David wrote in the Psalms, "Praise the Lord, my soul, and forget not all his benefits—who forgives all your sins and heals all your diseases" (Psalm 103:2–3 NIV). Healing is in God's benefits package!

The great evangelist T. L. Osborn said, "If it is not God's will for you to be well, it would be wrong for you to seek recovery even through natural means. If it is God's will for you to be well, then it is only logical that the best way of recovery is by divine means."[26]

Here are a few Scriptures and realities that show it is God's will to heal:

HEALING IS IN GOD'S NATURE

In Exodus 15:26 God revealed Himself to Israel as "The Lord Who Heals." Healing is not just something God does; healing is in His nature. God is a Healer. It's fitting that Jesus, God made flesh—the invisible God made visible—came demonstrating this same healing nature.

> Jesus went throughout Galilee, teaching in their synagogues, proclaiming the good news of the kingdom, and healing every disease and sickness among the people.
>
> Matthew 4:23 NIV

HEALING IS IN GOD'S KINGDOM

When Jesus taught His disciples to pray, He said to pray like this:

> "Our Father in heaven, hallowed be Your name. *Your kingdom come.* Your will be done *on earth as it is in heaven.*"
>
> Matthew 6:9–10

Simply put, God wants heaven to invade earth. Jesus asked us to pray that His kingdom would come on earth as it is in heaven. There's no sickness or pain in heaven, so one of the manifestations of heaven on earth is healing ministry.

> **When the kingdom shows up, healing comes with it.**

When the kingdom shows up, healing comes with it. The kingdom of God takes dominion over sickness, pain, and disease. The message of the kingdom is: There's a new King in town and He reigns and dominates over every sickness, disease, and torment. Sickness, go! Healing come.

Jesus told His disciples in Luke 10:9, "Heal the sick who are there and tell them, 'The kingdom of God has come near to you'" (NIV).

HEALING IS IN JESUS' EXAMPLE

> Then Jesus went about all the cities and villages, teaching in their synagogues, preaching the gospel of the kingdom, and healing every sickness and every disease among the people.
>
> Matthew 9:35

Epilepsy, the paralyzed, leprosy, fever, excessive blood flow, blind, mute, deaf, withered hand, a lady whose back wouldn't straighten—Jesus healed them all!

> Then great multitudes came to Him, having with them the lame, blind, mute, maimed, and many others; and they laid them down at Jesus' feet, and He healed them.
>
> Matthew 15:30

> And the whole multitude sought to touch Him, for power went out from Him and healed them all.
>
> Luke 6:19

As the Scriptures above prove, healing was a normal part of Jesus' ministry.

Some people think, "Well, that was Jesus, healing is not for us." Jesus is our example! We were meant to follow Him into His healing ministry just as the early disciples did. We are also disciples of Jesus. Disciples follow the example of the one they follow.

Jesus said, "Most assuredly, I say to you, he who believes in Me, *the works that I do he will do also*; and greater works than these he will do, because I go to My Father" (John 14:12).

This is why we need the power of the Holy Spirit in our lives. When we are baptized in the Holy Spirit, we are clothed with God's ability.

God Wants to Use You to Heal

It's important to know that God wants to heal people, but it's also important to know that God wants to use *you* to bring healing. One of the signs that accompanies believers is that they lay hands on the sick and the sick recover (Mark 16:18). If you're a believer, then you're qualified to bring healing!

Since that's true, what should you do to prepare yourself? Firstly, I want to encourage you to expand what you think is possible. Nothing is impossible for God, and nothing is impossible for the person who believes (Mark 9:23, Luke 1:37). God can use you to do wild miracles! Yes, you!

When Jesus said that the ones who believe in Him will do the works that He's been doing, that should make you stop and think about His works. He walked on water, multiplied food, raised the dead, healed the sick, and more. The second part of the verse says we will do "greater works than" the ones Jesus performed (John 14:12).

I'm saying this to stir you to expand what you think is possible. Ask yourself, *What could God do through me?*

> **God is still healing today, and He wants to use you to do it.**

Secondly, you need to upgrade your normal. If you were to insert your life into the book of Acts, would you be a normal Christian or an abnormal one? Maybe it's time for an upgrade!

Bill Johnson said, "You know your mind is renewed when the impossible looks logical."[27]

I remember years ago watching an evangelist on YouTube bring healing as he ministered on the streets. He prayed for many who had uneven leg lengths, where one leg was shorter than the other, and the short leg grew out to match the other leg. I watched so many of those videos that my mind got renewed to believe that growing out uneven legs was normal.[28] Since then, I've seen this miracle many times in my ministry.

When I was a youth pastor, one of my students had a short right leg. From playing soccer, his hips got out of alignment and caused his right leg to be shorter. We prayed for him, and his leg shot out and became even. He went back to his chiropractor not long after and he told the young man that he didn't need to adjust him because his legs were already even.

Imagine what kind of mindset Peter and John had when they walked up to the Gate Beautiful, commanded a crippled man to walk, grabbed him by the hand and lifted him up, and the man was miraculously healed (Acts 3:1–10). Healing is normal in the kingdom of God. Elevate the way you think to the way of the kingdom.

Thirdly, believe. God is still healing today, and He wants to use you to do it. Faith is the only prerequisite.

Here are a few practical things you can do to prepare yourself for healing ministry:

MEDITATE ON THE WORD

Years ago, I went on a mission trip to Uganda and for some months leading up to the trip, I meditated specifically on multiple Scriptures that spoke of God's healing power. Joshua 1:8 tells us that when we "meditate" on the Word, we would follow the Word and "have good success."

Meditating on the Word gets the truth in you and renews your mind to God's perspective. In other words, it helps you to think like God. Imagine being around Jesus' healing ministry regularly and seeing people getting healed consistently. That would do something to the way you think. That's what meditating on the Word does: It gets you a front-row seat to a move of God.

On that trip, my friend and I prayed for a lady who was crippled. She didn't have a wheelchair, so she scooted her way up to the front for prayer. After prayer, I asked her to do something she couldn't do, and she got up on her once crippled legs and started leaping in praise to God!

FEED ON TESTIMONIES

Testimonies take the theological and make it practical. Testimonies show God in action. Hearing testimonies, just like meditating on the Word, shifts the way we think.

I encourage you to search out and feed on the testimonies of what God has done, starting in Scripture and going through history up to the present day. God is a miracle working God and taking time to meditate on testimonies will elevate your mindset and faith.

The testimonies of what God has done train us to expect the same miracles. Charles Spurgeon said, "What he has done once, is a prophecy of what he intends to do again."[29]

GET AROUND THOSE WHO FLOW IN HEALING

The word anointing comes from a Hebrew word that means "to smear."[30] When you're around others who walk in the healing anointing, that anointing smears or "rubs off" on you.

Proverbs 13:20 says, in essence, that you become like the people you hang around. Get around people who walk in greater anointings than you and let those anointings influence you. If you can't get to them in person, there are all kinds of resources like YouTube that allow you to sit under those who are further along in their walks with the Lord.

It's like going to a coffee shop. If you're in there long enough, the smell of coffee gets on you and you carry that wherever you go. It's been said many times, "The anointing is more caught than taught." Get around anointed ministries that walk in healing and you will catch the anointing.

Ways That Healing Flows

Here are a few practical ways that healing flows through believers.

LAYING ON OF HANDS

Jesus said that believers will "lay hands on the sick, and they will recover" (Mark 16:18). Our hands were meant to be conduits through which God's power flows.

> When the sun was setting, all those who had any that were sick with various diseases brought them to Him; and He laid His hands on every one of them and healed them.
>
> Luke 4:40

One Easter Sunday at church, I got to pray for a lady who needed healing for her tennis elbow. After her elbow got healed, she asked for prayer for the passageway to her stomach. She had a hard time swallowing for months and food would get stuck. Eating made her fearful because she did not know if she would choke. After prayer, I told her to eat something, but I never got to see the result, because my family and I left to spend time together after the service. She came back a few weeks later and testified that she could eat freely now because the Lord healed her!

If you want to see people get healed, lay hands on them!

WORDS OF KNOWLEDGE

I began to share about this in the last chapter. A word of knowledge, regarding healing, is when God supernaturally shows you something that needs healing in someone's body.

I was leading worship in Bakersfield, California, one time, and the

Lord gave me a word of knowledge about healing learning disabilities. I spoke it out, declared healing, and then moved on. Months later, a mother came and testified about her son who had battled auditory dyslexia. They had seen improvements over the years, but that night he received the word, and everything shifted. His mother and he knew he was healed, and the healing was further displayed by his significant improvement in school. This young man has graduated high school, gone to ministry school, and carries the power of God.

In the same way you practiced hearing God in the last chapter, practice listening for words of knowledge. When words of knowledge come, they boost the faith of both the recipient and the person with the word.

I've found that when I'm led by the Spirit, whether with a word of knowledge or a sense in my spirit, I see better results. This is explained by what Jesus said in John 5:19, "Most assuredly, I say to you, the Son can do nothing of Himself, but what He sees the Father do; for whatever He does, the Son also does in like manner."

COMMANDING PRAYER

One thing you see in the Gospels and book of Acts is that Jesus and the disciples didn't pray for people to get healed; they commanded them to be healed. In other words, they didn't ask God to do it, they used the authority that God gave them and commanded healing.

This is a major shift in the way many people today approach healing ministry, but it's a needed one.

Authority is part of our function in the kingdom of God. We use the authority Jesus gave us to heal the sick, and as representatives of Christ, we command healing to come and diseases and pain to get out.

I am not saying you can't ask God in prayer for Him to heal people. I'm just saying the usual pattern for healing in the New Testament was concise commands.

There are many ways healing comes. Here are a few examples:

- A word (Psalm 107:20; Matthew 8:8)
- A prophetic act (2 Kings 5:10, 14; John 9:7)
- Anointing with oil (Mark 6:13; James 5:14)
- Casting a demon out (We'll get to that in the next chapter.)
- A handkerchief or shadow! (Acts 5:15; 19:12)

All these types of healing come through faith and God honors faith.

Just Do It

The best way to learn about healing ministry is to just do it. You can start at your church, small group, neighborhood, family gatherings, on the streets, or wherever you go!

You may be walking in a crowded area and you see someone with crutches or a brace, that's a candidate for the healing power of God! You may be at your small group during worship and get a picture of someone's shoulder in pain. Ask the leader if you can ask if there is someone present with that symptom in the room and if you can pray for them. You may be talking to one of your neighbors and the Lord shows you that their neck is in pain. Ask if that person deals with any pain in that area and pray for them.

God wants to reveal Himself to the people around you and healing is one way He does this.

That being said, here are some practical steps to take when ministering healing. I've taken a bit from Randy Clark's Five Step Prayer Model and made it my own. [31]

> **The best way to learn about healing ministry is to just do it.**

INTERVIEW

- Ask them what they need healing for.
    - "What do you need healing for?"
- Ask them if the word of knowledge you received applies to them.
    - "Do you need healing in your shoulder?"
- Ask what level of pain they are in
    - "On a scale of 1–10, 10 being the most pain, what number are you at?"
    - I ask that so I can gauge where they're at and have a point of reference for improvement.

PRAYER

- Ask if you can lay hands on the person where the pain is if this is appropriate or lay hands on their shoulder.
- Command the pain or sickness to go in Jesus' name.
- Invite healing to come in Jesus' name.
    - "I command that pain to go out of their shoulder. I release healing right now, be healed in Jesus' name."

INTERVIEW AGAIN

- Have them do something to see if the pain has decreased or gone.
    - "Test it out. Do something you couldn't do before."
    - "If you were at a 7 before, what number are you at now?"
- If they are healed 100% no more pain, praise God!
- If the pain has decreased, but still needs more healing, praise God! Pray again and believe that God will finish what He has started.
    - "Father, thank You that You began something here. I ask You now to complete what You started. In Jesus' name, I command this shoulder to be completely healed."
    - Then interview again.

When people get healed, use it as an opportunity to share the gospel with them. If they're already believers, encourage them that God loves them, sees them, and is with them.

Something to remember is that people can't always check if they've been healed. For example, there may not be sensory evidence if a person has been healed from a blood disease or an internal organ injury. In these moments, you just trust God to do the work and leave it with Him and encourage the person. Sometimes people come back after they have taken tests and they let you know the results.

You may ask, "What happens if people don't get healed?" Sometimes this happens. Our job is to believe God and trust Him to do what we cannot do. We do not shame or blame people for not getting healed. Other times, people don't get healed on the spot, but they get healed the next day. Sometimes there are other things at play, such as demonic influence. Then your prayer is not a healing prayer, it is a deliverance prayer. We'll get to that in the next chapter.

Overall, we do our part, which is to have faith, lay hands, and pray. We can trust that God will do His part.

One thing I know for sure is, if you never pray for the sick, you'll never see them get healed. But the more you step out in faith and begin to pray for the sick, the more you will see them get healed!

Here's my word for you: God is going to do amazing things through you! Get ready to see healing miracles begin to break out all around you.

Activation

SMALL GROUP ACTIVATION

In a small group setting, like a youth group, home fellowship, or family gathering, take time to minister in healing. Ask the group if anyone has pain or sickness that they need healing for. Once the people needing healing are identified, join together as a group and lay hands on them and pray.

You can also take time to ask God for words of knowledge for healing. Ask if anyone present has the condition that your word of knowledge identifies. Then pray for that person and release healing!

Use the steps above as a guide for healing ministry.

Chapter 7

Deliverance

> And these signs will follow those who believe:
> In My name they will cast out demons.
>
> The Lord Jesus, Mark 16:17

As you step into a life of power that points to Jesus, you're going to run into demons. And it's our job as believers to cast them out. I'm not talking about going demon hunting. I'm saying, that as you seek to make Jesus known and help people, inevitably there will be times that someone needs a demon cast out of them. Jesus rules over every demon and has given us the authority to cast them out and bring deliverance!

We live in a spiritual world. There is light and darkness and there are angels and demons. The devil—once an angel—got kicked out of heaven and took a third of the angels with him. These are now demons. They are evil spirits whose goal is to wreak havoc in people's lives and draw people away from Christ. The good news is that God wants to kick demons out of people and set people free!

One time, a young adult came up to my wife and I during altar ministry and said she had a recent dream where we were praying over her, and I was waving my hand a bit intensely. Now, I had just preached a message on the power of the blood of Jesus and invited people to the front for prayer. Prior to her telling us her dream, another girl had just manifested a demon and we prayed for her. So, I just knew we were about to go into round two.

We started praying for this woman and I felt led to ask her if there was anybody she needed to forgive. She said yes and so we led her in a prayer of forgiveness. When it came to the part where she was supposed to forgive, she couldn't get the word "forgive" out, and began choking. I knew we were dealing with a spirit here, so I bound the demon and commanded it to loose her tongue. She got the word out, forgave the one whom she held an offense against, and the demon left. Then we prayed that God would fill her up with His Spirit and His peace.

The good news is that Jesus defeated the devil at the cross and in His resurrection. We get to enforce that victory (Colossians 2:14–15; Hebrews 2:14). God wants to set people free and use you to do it!

Deliverance is Normal in the Kingdom

Casting demons out was a normal part of Jesus' ministry and in His disciples' ministries.

> When evening had come, they brought to Him many who were demon-possessed. And He cast out the spirits with a word, and healed all who were sick.
>
> Matthew 8:16

> As they went out, behold, they brought to Him a man, mute and demon-possessed. And when the demon was cast out, the mute spoke. And the multitudes marveled, saying, "It was never seen like this in Israel!"
>
> Matthew 9:32–33

> But Jesus rebuked him, saying, "Be quiet, and come out of him!" And when the unclean spirit had convulsed him and cried out with a loud voice, he came out of him.
>
> Mark 1:25–26

It was even normal with His disciples:

> And they cast out many demons, and anointed with oil many who were sick, and healed them.
>
> Mark 6:13

> Then the seventy returned with joy, saying, "Lord, even the demons are subject to us in Your name."
>
> Luke 10:17

Deliverance is part of kingdom ministry. Like healing, when the kingdom comes, demons get kicked out!

> "But if I cast out demons with the finger of God, surely the kingdom of God has come upon you."
>
> Luke 11:20

> "But if I cast out demons by the Spirit of God, surely the kingdom of God has come upon you."
>
> Matthew 12:28

Jesus said in Matthew 24:14, "And this gospel of the kingdom will be preached in all the world as a witness to all the nations, and then the end will come." The end hasn't come yet, so the gospel of the kingdom is still in employment! If the kingdom is still coming, then the demons are still getting kicked out. If you've ever needed convincing that the Christian life is supernatural, just start ministering in deliverance. You will learn quickly that there is more than meets the eye. The good news is that Jesus is King over all, and the unseen realm submits to the name of Jesus.

> And these signs will follow those who believe: In My name they will cast out demons.
>
> Mark 16:17

As followers of Jesus, we have been given authority from the Lord Jesus to cast out demons.

Live Prepared

Like I said before, as you step into a life of power, you are going to run into demons. Your first encounter with a demon is not the time to get yourself ready for battle! You want to live prepared.

Here are a few tips to help you live prepared for deliverance:

KNOW WHO YOU ARE

In Acts 19, there is a story of a deliverance gone wrong.

> Then some of the itinerant Jewish exorcists took it upon themselves to call the name of the Lord Jesus over those who had evil spirits, saying, "We exorcise you by the Jesus whom Paul preaches." Also there were seven sons of Sceva, a Jewish chief priest, who did so. And the evil spirit answered and said, "Jesus I know, and Paul I know; but who are you?"

Then the man in whom the evil spirit was leaped on them, overpowered them, and prevailed against them, so that they fled out of that house naked and wounded.

Acts 19:13–16

People would probably say the seven sons of Sceva were not saved, which is why the devil could attack the way he did. This is probably the case, but I want to present to you a different angle. What if the sons of Sceva were saved, but the demon's question caused them to doubt who they were? What if the devil is trying to get you to question who you are?

> **As followers of Jesus, we have been given authority from the Lord Jesus to cast out demons.**

I remember taking Spanish in community college and the professor asked me to say a phrase in Spanish. I did. Then he asked me, "Are you sure?" And because I wasn't fully convinced of what I said, his question only worked to make me doubt myself more. *I don't know, am I sure*, I thought. My Spanish teacher was a good man, so I doubt he was *trying* to make me doubt myself. However, the enemy *wants* you to doubt your identity in the Lord. He wants to convince you that you do not have authority and are not a child of God.

This is why it is so important to know who you are. The sons of Sceva either were not in Christ, or they did not know who they were in Christ and things did not end well for them. I don't say this to make you afraid, but to encourage you to know who you are in Christ.

What does God say about you? Scripture says you are loved, forgiven, set free, anointed, and blessed. You have been given authority in the name of Jesus, "Greater is He that is in you than He that is in the world" (1 John 4:4 NASB95). You can "do all things through Christ who strengthens [you]" (Philippians 4:13). You are more than a conqueror through Him who loves you (Romans 8:37). And as Isaiah 54:17 says, "No weapon formed against you shall prosper."

> Behold, I give you the authority to trample on serpents and scorpions, and over all the power of the enemy, and nothing shall by any means hurt you.
>
> Luke 10:19

Let these truths settle on the inside. Walk in your authority and identity in Christ. Don't let the devil push you around.

BE A PERSON OF PRAYER

In another deliverance story from Scripture, the disciples were trying to cast a demon out of a boy but couldn't. Jesus rebuked the demon and cast it out. And then the disciples came to Jesus and said, "'Why could we not cast it out?' So He said to them, 'This kind can come out by nothing but prayer and fasting'" (Mark 9:28–29).

> " **Jesus demonstrated that a life of prayer is a life of power.**

It's interesting to me that Jesus points to prayer and fasting as the key to breakthrough in this situation. It's not as if Jesus had time to go away and pray and fast; instead, He lived a lifestyle of prayer and fasting. Jesus prioritized His prayer life. Jesus demonstrated that a life of prayer is a life of power.

I don't think Jesus had a prophetic word that said, "In this many days, you will encounter a boy that needs deliverance, so get ready and pray and fast so you'll be prepared to cast the demon out." That could have happened, but I think more likely Jesus just loved spending time with His Father and catching His heart. Prayer hooks you into the heart of God and prepares you for the work of God.

> Then Jesus answered and said to them, "Most assuredly, I say to you, the Son can do nothing of Himself, but what He sees the Father do; for whatever He does, the Son also does in like manner."
>
> John 5:19

I believe this verse comes from a lifestyle of prayer.

When it comes to fasting, be led by the Lord. Jesus said, "*When* you fast" not "*if* you fast" (see Matthew 6:16–18). It's a normal part of a Christian's spiritual disciplines. Fasting is denying your flesh to build up your spirit. And Jesus makes it clear that fasting helps with deliverance ministry.

A prayerful life is a powerful life.

LIVE A SUBMITTED LIFE

> Therefore submit to God. Resist the devil and he will flee from you.
>
> James 4:7

Don't try to kick the devil out of someone if you are living in agreement with the devil! Repent of any known sin, submit to the lordship of Jesus, and live a holy life. Shut any doors you may have opened to the devil through sin. Ephesians 4:27 says, "Do not give the devil a foothold" (NIV). Don't give him any opportunity!

Jesus spoke of the devil and said "he has nothing in Me" (John 14:30).

For Jesus, there was no landing place for the devil.

James 4:6 says, "God resists the proud, but gives grace to the humble". Stay humble. Years ago, there was a man I knew who became prideful because he had cast a bunch of demons out. He started calling himself the "demon demolisher." Shortly after that, he got super sick with malaria and had to humble himself before the Lord. It was a lesson to "not think of yourself more highly than you ought" (Romans 12:3 NIV). We need to stay humble and remember it's Jesus' name and authority that the demons submit to.

Staying humble is not only so that we can cast demons out, it is just good for your walk with the Lord.

Seek Discernment

> But the manifestation of the Spirit is given to each one for the profit of all…to another discerning of spirits.
>
> 1 Corinthians 12:7, 10

One of the gifts of the Spirit that you're going to want to seek after is the gift of discerning of spirits. This gift gives you the ability to discern or know the spirit behind an action or condition. Important to note: the gift of discernment is not the "gift" of suspicion or accusation. Remember, love believes the best of every person (1 Corinthians 13:7 AMPC).

We used to live in a house that was next to a large field. I had made a pile of rocks near the hose outlet and one day I went over there, moved a rock, and a snake jumped out. Snakes like rocks and hot places and I realized the reason it was there was because I created a dwelling place for it. People get demons because there is a dwelling place or open door for them. Open doors can open due to unhealed abuse and trauma, unforgiveness, sexual immorality, witchcraft, and other sinful things.

One question you want to be asking the Lord when confronted with someone demonized is, "What is the open door? How did this demon get here?"

One time I was praying for a lady and training a young adult in healing ministry. We had ministered healing in a prayer line, and once we got to a certain lady, she said she had been dealing with headaches. I felt in my spirit, or discerned, that this wasn't just a physical problem; this was spiritual.

I told the young adult that I was training that this is not healing ministry now, this is deliverance ministry. I asked the lady a few questions. "Do you or anyone in your family do witchcraft?" She said yes, someone in her family. "Are they mad at you?" She said yes. I told the lady that the headaches have come because her family members are putting witchcraft on her and we were going to break that witchcraft off. I led her in a forgiveness prayer to forgive those who hurt her and then rebuked the witchcraft off of her and the headaches left.

In this situation, I was using the gift of discernment to get to the root of the issue. Healing prayer would not have worked because we were not praying for healing. We were casting a demon of affliction out.

There have been other times when I have prayed for someone who had pain in a certain place of his or her body. I started praying and the pain moves. Then I moved my hand to the other spot and the pain moves again. This is a clear sign that the issue is not physical, it's spiritual. The demon was moving around in the person's body trying to get away from the power of God. I switched from healing ministry to deliverance ministry and cast that demon out! Then the pain left.

The reason why it's important to ask for the gift of discernment is so we don't waste time praying the wrong prayers and nothing gets done. We want to know what is going on so we can be effective in ministry.

Getting Practical

Here's a scenario. Someone approaches you for prayer at church, you start praying and a demon manifests. What do you do?

Something important to consider: Does the person want to be free? Do they have any intention of following Jesus? You may want to reconsider casting the demons out if the answer to these questions is no.

If they don't surrender to the Lord Jesus, then "seven spirits more wicked than [the original evil spirit]" will come back with the one that was cast out (Matthew 12:43–45 NIV). You don't want to make it worse for them.

It is possible that once they're delivered, they would then want to follow Jesus (see Mark 5:18–20). I just want to mention this as something to keep in mind.

In this section, I'm going to walk through some practical steps to take when casting out demons.

OVERALL, LOVE THE PERSON

Treat the person with kindness. Don't expose them in front of people. First Peter 4:8 says, "Above all, love each other deeply, because love covers a multitude of sins" (NIV). You may want to take the person aside so people are not staring at him or her wondering what's going on. You don't want to embarrass the person, you want to cover him or her.

> **The walk of power is a walk of love.**

You have to remember that this person is not your ministry project. They are a real person that needs the love of God. The walk of power is a walk of love.

USE YOUR AUTHORITY IN CHRIST

Jesus gave us His name. His name carries all authority. At the name of Jesus, "every knee will bow" (Philippians 2:10 NASB95). When you speak in Jesus' name, and according to His will, His authority is backing you.

DISCERN THE MANIFESTATIONS

Let's talk about manifestations for a moment. How do you know if a demon is manifesting? This is where your relationship with the Holy Spirit and the gift of discernment kicks in. But there are some common signs there is a demon manifesting such as screaming, growling, excessive sighing, groaning, or weeping, pain, ailments, coughing, contortions, or the person's voice changes.

Sometimes it's obvious there's a demon and other times it's not. This is a good place to say that not everything is a demon! Use discernment, ask the Holy Spirit, and be kind. You can always ask the person what is going on with them.

Why do demons manifest? They want attention. They want to make a scene. They want to intimidate you and the people nearby. It's their last effort to try to shake you of your authority. That's why I shut down the manifestations and don't allow the devil to put on a show.

BIND THE DEMON

Once I identify that a demon is present, I usually bind it and command it to be quiet. Jesus usually shut down the demons from talking (see Mark 1:25, 34). I do this because, as I mentioned earlier, I do not want the person to be embarrassed. I also do not want to give the devil a platform to grab everyone's attention.

I also want to work with the person for their freedom. It's important they are along for the process. One thing I've found that helps, especially in tougher cases, is that I work to maintain eye contact. If I can keep eye contact with the person, the person stays present and the demon stays bound. Demons do not like eye contact with believers because they hate Christ's light shining through our eyes.

When the person is present, it is easier to get to the root of the issue.

IDENTIFY THE ROOT ISSUE

What is the open door? How did the demon get here?

Ask the Holy Spirit to give you discernment. Ask the person questions. You can also invite the person to pray and ask the Lord how the demon got there.

I've found that many times unforgiveness has opened the door for a demon to come and torment the person. Jesus told a parable in Matthew 18:21–35 about an unforgiving servant who got turned over to tormentors. I believe these tormentors represent demons. They come and torment the unforgiving person. However, once the individual forgives, the tormentors must let them go.

Whatever the root is, once you identify it, you can deal with it.

DEAL WITH THE ROOT ISSUE

You deal with the root issue through repenting, renouncing, and forgiving.

If their problem was unforgiveness, remind them of Christ's forgiveness through the cross and lead them in a prayer of forgiveness to those who hurt them.

If their problem was sin, remind them of Christ's forgiveness through the cross and their need to repent. Lead them in a prayer of repentance.

Repentance is turning from sin and turning to God.

If their problem was witchcraft, remind them of Christ's forgiveness through the cross and their need to repent. Lead them in a prayer of repentance, renouncing witchcraft, and receiving forgiveness.

To renounce means to give up by formal declaration.[32] In the case of witchcraft, renouncing is announcing that you have nothing to do with that practice anymore. In any case, it's important to break any agreement with the devil that the person may have had.

CAST IT OUT!

By this point, the demon may have already left. Once the demon has no landing place or hook, they sometimes leave right away, but other times they are stubborn. That's when you use your authority in Christ and command the demon to go. It could be as simple as, "In Jesus' name, I command you to come out!"

It's important to note that voice volume doesn't equal authority. The devil recognizes the authority of Jesus regardless of volume. Sometimes your volume increases when you assert your authority.

There's a story of the late revivalist, Smith Wigglesworth that illustrates how to deal with the devil.

> Once in England Smith Wigglesworth was standing on a street corner waiting for a bus. A woman came out of an apartment house, and a little dog ran out behind her. She said, "Honey, you're going to have to go back."
>
> The dog didn't pay any attention to her. He just wagged his tail and rubbed up against her affectionately.
>
> She said, "Now, dear, you can't go." The little dog wagged his tail and rubbed up against her again.
>
> About that time, the bus arrived. The woman stomped her foot and yelled, "Get!" The dog tucked his tail between his legs and took off.
>
> Wigglesworth said he hollered out loud with even thinking, "That's the way you've got to do with the devil!"[33]

Assert your authority in Christ. Don't be passive. Authority also doesn't equal being mean. Treat the person with kindness; treat the devil with sternness. If the demon remains stubborn and doesn't leave, you may want to take a cue from the way this lady treated her disobedient dog, or you may want to revisit discerning the root issue.

How do you know the demon is gone? Ask the Holy Spirit, use the gift of discernment, and ask the person if it left. Is the torment gone? Is the pain gone?

FILL THE PERSON WITH THE HOLY SPIRIT

Once the demon(s) leave the person, ask God to fill him or her up with the Holy Spirit.

> "When an unclean spirit goes out of a man, he goes through dry places, seeking rest, and finds none. Then he says, 'I will return to my house from which I came.' And when he comes, he finds it empty, swept, and put in order. Then he goes and takes with him seven other spirits more wicked than himself, and they enter and dwell there; and the last state of that man is worse than the first. So shall it also be with this wicked generation."
>
> Matthew 12:43–45

This Scripture implies that no one took over the house once the demons left. You don't want seven more demons coming back and finding an empty place. You want to set the person up for sustained freedom. How do you do this?

If the person isn't saved, lead them to Christ. Lead them in a simple prayer of repentance and surrender to Jesus as their Lord.

If they are saved, invite them to surrender to the Lord Jesus afresh. Lead them in a simple prayer of surrender to Jesus as Lord of their life. Some people might have a problem with this because I'm saying that Christians can have a demon. In my experience, I've seen it happen with people that I've known to be born-again followers of Jesus who needed deliverance. How does that happen? If Jesus lives in their heart or spirit, the demon may be occupying their body or soul.

Whatever the case, after they have surrendered their lives to Jesus, invite the Holy Spirit to occupy the territory the demon once had. I'd invite them to receive the baptism of the Holy Spirit with the evidence of speaking in tongues.

POST DELIVERANCE SUGGESTIONS

Encourage the person to get rid of anything that associated them with the sin or the open door to the demon. For example, in Acts 19, former occultists burned their witchcraft books.

> And many who had believed came confessing and telling their deeds. Also, many of those who had practiced magic brought their books together and burned them in the sight of all. And they counted up the value of them, and it totaled fifty thousand pieces of silver. So the word of the Lord grew mightily and prevailed.
>
> Acts 19:18–20

This is a lot of magic books; 50,000 pieces of silver's worth. That amount of money in our day equals several million dollars. Millions of dollars' worth of books that corrupted an entire city by opening the door to darkness were willingly burned up and turned to ashes. How about that for shutting the door to darkness!

Whatever it may be—witchcraft books, pornography, objects that are connected to a past relationship, emails, text messages, the list could go on—encourage the person who was set free to throw those objects away or delete those messages. If someone gets delivered from alcohol, they shouldn't go back to hang out at a bar! The devil will tempt them to go back to their past, the same way the Israelites were tempted to go back to Egypt. The bottom line is, urge the person to not go back to the same demon that bound them.

Encourage them to seek the Lord and His truth. Get them connected to a church if they aren't already. Encourage the person to get in the Word, pray, worship, and seek godly fellowship. Encourage them to find Scripture that tells them the truth about their situation. In other words, get them some good discipleship. You want them to not only get free but stay free.

Maybe It's Just One Step

You may end up skipping all these steps and just command the demon to come out! Then get them saved and/or filled with the Holy Spirit. I've just learned over time that these steps can be helpful.

There were some people in the Gospels, like Mary Magdalene and the unnamed man possessed by a legion, who were so touched by the power and love of God that they became devoted followers of Jesus. My guess is they didn't go through all the above steps but Jesus just delivered them, and they followed Him.

> Now it came to pass, afterward, that He went through every city and village, preaching and bringing the glad tidings of the kingdom of God. And the twelve were with Him, and certain women who had been healed of evil spirits and infirmities—Mary called Magdalene, out of whom had come seven demons.
>
> Luke 8:1–2

> Then they came to Jesus, and saw the one who had been demon-possessed and had the legion, sitting and clothed and in his right mind... And when He got into the boat, he who had been demon-possessed begged Him that he might be with Him. However, Jesus did not permit him, but said to him, "Go home to your friends, and tell them what great things the

Lord has done for you, and how He has had compassion on you." And he departed and began to proclaim in Decapolis all that Jesus had done for him; and all marveled.

Mark 5:15, 18–20

While the above steps do not *have* to be followed to bring deliverance, I trust these practical steps are helpful. Overall, follow the Holy Spirit and share the power and love of God with people who need freedom.

In Conclusion

Let's recap the practical steps:

- Love the person
- Use your authority in Christ
- Discern the manifestations
- Bind the demon
- Identify the root issue
- Deal with the root issue
- Cast it out!
- Fill the person with the Holy Spirit
- Post deliverance suggestions

For yourself, remember the keys to living prepared—know who you are, be a person of prayer, and live a submitted life. This will not only help before deliverance ministry, but afterward.

Deliverance ministry continues today because God still wants to set people free! Jesus is Lord, He lives in you and wants to move through you!

Activation

Here is a prayer of faith to activate you in the ministry of deliverance:

> Lord Jesus, You are the Lord of all. Your name is above every name, and You rule over the devil and every demon. I thank You that You have defeated the devil and that You have given me authority to cast out demons in Your name. I ask You to fill me with Your love and for the gift of discernment. Let Your kingdom come, and Your will be done in and through my life. I submit to You, God, and resist the devil, and he will flee from me. Use me for Your glory to set people free, in Jesus' name!

I do not recommend searching for demons, but if a demon manifests or if you discern one, now you have some equipping to cast it out!

Chapter 8

Preach the Gospel

> For God so loved the world that He gave His only begotten Son, that whoever believes in Him should not perish but have everlasting life.
>
> John 3:16

One of my grandmothers passed due to Covid in December 2021. She was a fun-loving grandmother who was always so supportive. I got to officiate her memorial service the following January and something significant happened.

The day of the memorial service, I woke up and heard the Lord say, "Contend for souls," and I saw a picture of myself on my face in prayer. Well, while getting ready and getting our boys ready to go, I totally forgot to take heed of what God had said but I knew I was supposed to take some time and cry out to God in prayer for souls to be saved.

I remembered what the Lord had said on the drive over to the service and told my wife. I grabbed her hand, and we began to pray. Immediately, I saw a vision of this long, thin cliff and people were falling from it. I began to weep. I hadn't felt that kind of compassion for souls in a long time. Even just thinking of that moment moves me. The vision revealed that these people were falling to their deaths without Jesus.

In the vision, I saw myself wearing a suit and catching people who were falling and pulling them back up. I knew that my assignment was to pull people back up through the preaching of the gospel at this service. My wife and I prayed and believed God for souls. It's hard to describe in words, but it was like the Lord gave me His heart for people and the urgency of this opportunity.

We had a great time at the service remembering Grammy and then came time to share the gospel message. Some people might think it's tacky to preach the gospel at a funeral, but honestly, it's one of the best opportunities because people are confronted with the reality of death. I remained aware while delivering the message that we were there for a memorial, but you best bet that Grammy—who was in heaven's glory with Jesus—would've wanted people to hear the gospel! While I endeavored to honor the tone and purpose of the service, I still fulfilled the assignment from the Lord.

I shared about the glories of heaven and how, to the believer, death is a momentary transition to everlasting life. I shared John 3:16 and Romans 6:23, which says, "For the wages of sin is death, but the free gift of God is eternal life through Christ Jesus our Lord." (NLT). Then I invited people to receive Jesus and eternal life and a handful of people prayed to accept the Lord!

Praise God! Based on that vision the Lord showed me, people were rescued from falling to their deaths without Jesus.

The greatest miracle is salvation. Our walk of power is meant to lead people to Jesus. We need to preach the gospel!

In this chapter, we're going to look at the gift of salvation and how to preach the gospel.

What is Salvation?

> For I am not ashamed of the gospel, because it is the power of God that brings salvation to everyone who believes: first to the Jew, then to the Gentile.
>
> Romans 1:16 NIV

The gospel of salvation is the message that Jesus rescues us from sin and darkness and gives us forgiveness and right relationship with God.

We were created by God and meant to have a relationship with Him. However, we "all have sinned and fall short of the glory of God" (Romans 3:23 NIV). The penalty for sin is death. Sin separates from God and there's no way back except through Christ.

> Jesus said to him, "I am the way, the truth, and the life. No one comes to the Father except through Me."
>
> John 14:6

> Salvation is found in no one else, for there is no other name under heaven given to mankind by which we must be saved.
>
> Acts 4:12 NIV

Jesus took all our sins on the cross, paid the penalty we all deserved, and made the way for us to be free and forgiven. His death was the sacrifice needed to take our sins away. The separation is done away with, and we can draw near to God.

For the wages of sin is death.

Romans 6:23

But God demonstrates His own love toward us in this: While we were still sinners, Christ died for us.

Romans 5:8 NIV

For Christ also suffered once for sins, the righteous for the unrighteous, to bring you to God.

1 Peter 3:18 NIV

> **Jesus took all our sins on the cross, paid the penalty we all deserved, and made the way for us to be free and forgiven.**

Jesus said we must be born-again (John 3:7); which tells me that our first birth falls short of the purpose of God. Our nature had been corrupted through sin. When we receive Christ into our lives, we become born again, or born of God. We become what the Bible calls "new creations." We receive a new nature!

> Yet to all who did receive Him, to those who believed in His name, He gave the right to become children of God—children born not of natural descent, nor of human decision or a husband's will, but born of God.

John 1:12–13 NIV

> Therefore, if anyone is in Christ, he is a new creation; old things have passed away; behold, all things have become new.

2 Corinthians 5:17

Through the gift of eternal life, our future rests secure in heaven.

> For God so loved the world that He gave His only begotten Son, that whoever believes in Him should not perish but have everlasting life.
>
> John 3:16

> For the wages of sin is death, but the gift of God is eternal life in Christ Jesus our Lord.
>
> Romans 6:23

Salvation is a gift! It's not because of our good works! We can't earn it; we can only receive it by faith.

> For it is by grace you have been saved, through faith—and this is not from yourselves, it is the gift of God—not by works, so that no one can boast.
>
> Ephesians 2:8–9 NIV

After Jesus was crucified, He was buried and on the third day, He rose back to life! He conquered sin, death, and the devil, and He's alive today and offers eternal life to all who would receive and believe!

Gospel literally means good news, and it is the greatest news of all time!

Paul said that the gospel is *the* power of God that brings salvation (see Romans 1:16). This word for "power" is the same word we've looked at earlier in this book—*dunamis.* This means that there is supernatural, dynamic, explosive, miracle-working power within the message of the gospel. The message itself carries power.

The gospel has the ability, or power, to put people into salvation. Which, as we have looked at, is the gift of forgiveness, freedom, and eternal life. Salvation, or being saved, means you're a new person made right with God.

Selah.

Meditate on this reality for a moment.

When I preach the gospel to people, I share briefly what I've shared here, and I boil salvation down to three things. If you accept Jesus, you can:

- Be forgiven of your sins
- Have a home in heaven
- Start a relationship with God

You may have heard it said that Christianity is not a religion, it's a relationship. It's true. Jesus said that eternal life is knowing God (John 17:3). When presenting the gospel, I always try to point people to a relationship with God.

Fishers of Men

> And Jesus, walking by the Sea of Galilee, saw two brothers, Simon called Peter, and Andrew his brother, casting a net into the sea; for they were fishermen. Then He said to them, "Follow Me, and I will make you fishers of men." They immediately left their nets and followed Him.
>
> Matthew 4:18–20

Now, I'm no expert in fishing, but I do know that fish don't just swarm around people and wait to be caught. You have to lure them in. You need to use bait. When I take our boys fishing in a nearby lake for bass, we always use live bait—shiners, or minnows. You can use worms or the little fake plastic things, but then you have to know what you're doing and work the bait. The live bait, however, always does the work for you! We usually catch some bass when we use the live bait, while the rest of the fishers at the lake come up empty.

All that to say, when you're preaching the gospel, the goal is to catch some people for God. And if fishing is the analogy that Jesus gave for doing that, we need to use some bait to draw people in!

I remember seeing a guy on the college campus near our church preaching hellfire and brimstone like he was from the 1950s. I referenced him in the first chapter. He drew a crowd—not because people were happy with his message, but because he was offending everyone, and they were angry. I was thinking, *The fish might've come around, but they for sure aren't biting!*

Somewhere along the way, people have picked up the idea that preaching hard, "telling it like it is," or confronting people harshly about their sin is the way to preach the gospel. I'm not saying we should compromise the truth, we definitely should hold fast to truth, but the *way* we bring the message has everything to do with how it is received. Paul said in Romans 2:4 that "the goodness of God leads you to repentance."

Do you think if my boys decided to splash around and make a bunch of noise, then the fish would come in droves? No way! They would be out of there fast! However, some good old-fashioned bait cast into the lake will draw them in. Harsh or angry preaching will drive people away. Remember our goal is to bring people to Christ, not drive them away from Him.

We would do well to follow the Golden Rule: "Do to others as you would have them do to you" (Luke 6:31 NIV). How would you want someone to preach the gospel to you? We all would probably appreciate a merciful tone, as opposed to harshness. Yes, sometimes we need a rude awakening, but *every time* we need the love of God.

What kind of "bait," then, should we use in preaching the gospel? Let's examine a few ways to minister the gospel as "fishers of men."

THE MESSAGE OF THE CROSS

People are drawn to the message of peace with God, forgiveness of sins, and sacrificial love. Everyone needs love. We just covered this in the last section, but it bears repeating: There is supernatural, dynamic, explosive, miracle-working power within the message of the gospel. The gospel is powerful!

> There is supernatural, dynamic, explosive, miracle-working power within the message of the gospel.

This powerful message is that Jesus died on the cross to forgive our sins, give us a home in heaven, and start a relationship with God. He did this because He loves us.

> This is love: not that we loved God, but that He loved us and sent His Son as an atoning sacrifice for our sins.
>
> 1 John 4:10 NIV

> But He was pierced for our transgressions, He was crushed for our iniquities; the punishment that brought us peace was on him, and by his wounds we are healed.
>
> Isaiah 53:5 NIV

There is so much to what Jesus did at the cross, we don't have room enough to describe it here. But I pray God gives you fresh revelation into Jesus' work at the cross! Ask God to reveal to you all that He's done at the cross.

Within this message, there is *dunamis*, explosive supernatural power. Don't be ashamed of the message. Share it boldly and freely because it has the power to change people's lives.

YOUR TESTIMONY

One of the best ways to share the gospel with people is to share with them how you came to know Christ. Testimonies can make the gospel personally applicable and relatable.

Three elements you want to cover when sharing your testimony are: before, how, and after.

For example, here's a brief summary of my testimony:

Before:

I didn't grow up going to church. I was skateboarding, partying, and doing ungodly things.

How:

As a teenager, two of my best friends wanted to take their lives two nights in a row. During that same time period, a man preached the gospel to me while I was at work. About a week after he shared with me, I got in a car accident on the freeway.

These events shocked me and made me want to find God. I went to a church that I was invited to by a friend. I kept encountering the love of God at church and when people would pray for me. I had never experienced a love like that before.

Over a period of six months of seeking, I finally surrendered my life to Christ.

Now:

Now I know I'm going to heaven. My sins are forgiven, I have a relationship with God, and I'm living in the purpose of God for my life!

HERE ARE A FEW POINTS TO HELP:

1. Be concise. Learn to share your testimony in about three minutes.
2. Don't dwell too much on the past. Point to Jesus.
3. Resist "Christianese." Use words the person can understand.
4. Be normal.
5. Highlight relevant moments. Different parts of your testimony will relate to different people. Follow the Spirit and pay attention to what's connecting with people.

When people hear how God did something for you, it gives them hope to believe He can do it for them too.

THE POWER OF GOD

Prophecy, healing, and words of knowledge, all the gifts mentioned in this book, are "bait" to bring people to Jesus.

Remember, Jesus said, "But you will receive power when the Holy Spirit comes on you; and you will be my witnesses" (Acts 1:8 NIV). A witness is someone who produces evidence. Not only does your testimony produce evidence, but the power of God demonstrated through your life produces evidence that Jesus is real.

My wife and I prayed for a girl who was serving us at a restaurant and her foot was healed of pain. We didn't just leave it there, we asked her if she knew if she was going to heaven when she died and she said she wasn't sure. We shared the gospel message with her, and she prayed in the restaurant to accept Jesus.

I find it's easier to preach Jesus to people once they've encountered His power and love through a miracle or prophecy. This is the whole point of this book: Walking in power that points people to Jesus!

> For our gospel did not come to you in word only,
> but also in power.
>
> 1 Thessalonians 1:5

There are so many ways we can help lead people to Jesus. With my church, we have done free food, concerts, giveaways, and showing love in practical ways, like helping people in need, giving money, and being kind people. No matter what bait you use, people need the gospel.

❝ The Holy Spirit loves the gospel!

You may have heard the phrase, "Preach the gospel at all times, if necessary, use words." I know the phrase intends to encourage people to live godly lives that point people to Jesus. That's good, but I just need to say it *is* necessary to use words!

> How, then, can they call on the one they have not believed in? And how can they believe in the one of whom they have not heard? And how can they hear without someone preaching to them?
>
> Romans 10:14 NIV

The Holy Spirit loves the gospel! When Peter was preaching the gospel at a guy named Cornelius' house, he said these words, "All the prophets testify about Him that everyone who believes in Him receives forgiveness of sins through His name." Look at the next verse, "While Peter was still speaking these words, the Holy Spirit came on all who heard the message" (Acts 10:43–44 NIV). He interrupted the sermon! It's like the Holy Spirit couldn't help Himself but come in power when the gospel message was being preached!

> **I find it's easier to preach Jesus to people once they've encountered His power and love through a miracle or prophecy.**

How to Preach the Gospel

So, how do you preach the gospel? How do you lead someone to Christ?

I remember the first time I led people to Jesus. I led two men to Christ on July 4th, 2004. I shared the message of the cross with them and then asked them if they wanted to receive Jesus. They said yes. I thought, *I've never gotten this far. What do I do next?* Now, I knew what to do, but this was exciting, and I was nervous. I led them the best I knew how, and they prayed to accept Jesus!

You may feel like you don't know what to do, but that's the point of this book. This book is meant to equip you to walk in power and share Jesus. As you step out and share Jesus, you'll find the best ways that work for you.

Here is a template you can use to preach the gospel.

The Message

Here are some points to cover while sharing the gospel:

GOD'S DESIRE

- To be in relationship with you
- To give you life and purpose

(John 3:16, John 10:10)

OUR PROBLEM

- We've all sinned
- No one's perfect
- Sin separates you from God
- Sin requires a penalty

(Romans 3:23, Isaiah 59:2, Romans 6:23)

GOD'S SOLUTION

- Jesus came and died on the cross for our sins
- He loved us and took the penalty we deserved
- So we could be free, forgiven, and reconnected with God and His purpose for our lives

(Romans 5:8, 1 Peter 2:24, 1 Peter 3:18)

OUR RESPONSE

- Repent from your sins
- Believe in Jesus and what He's done for you
- Confess that He is Lord and risen from the dead
- Follow Jesus

(Acts 2:38, 3:19, 16:31, Romans 10:9)

Use these points as a guide to share the gospel message. Put them into the conversation, mix in your own story, and be concise. Trust the Holy Spirit to move in their hearts.

The Invitation

Once you share the gospel message, invite them to receive Christ!

Ask the person you are talking to, "Do you want to receive Jesus? Do you want to give your life to Christ?"

Here is a sample prayer:

> "Lord Jesus, I come to You now. I ask You to forgive my sins. I believe You died on the cross for my sins, you were buried, and on the third day, You rose again. This day, I make You my Lord and Savior. I give You my life. I turn from my sins and turn to You. I receive Your forgiveness. I receive a brand-new start. I am now a follower of Jesus. In Jesus' name, amen."

After people accept Christ, I usually follow up that prayer with asking the Lord for the baptism in the Holy Spirit. I encourage them that they need the Holy Spirit to follow Jesus.

The Follow Up

CELEBRATE THEIR DECISION TO FOLLOW JESUS!

> In the same way, there is more joy in heaven over one lost sinner who repents and returns to God than over ninety-nine others who are righteous and haven't strayed away!
>
> Luke 15:7 NLT

ENCOURAGE THEM WITH SCRIPTURE ABOUT THEIR SALVATION.

> And this is the testimony: God has given us eternal life, and this life is in His Son. Whoever has the Son has life; whoever does not have the Son of God does not have life. I write these things to you who believe in the name of the Son of God so that you may know that you have eternal life.
>
> 1 John 5:11–13 NIV

ENCOURAGE THEM WITH KEYS ON HOW TO DEEPEN THEIR RELATIONSHIP WITH GOD, SUCH AS:

- Reading the Bible
- Praying daily
- Sharing Christ with others
- Finding a good church and building community with other believers

After that, you could exchange contact information to follow up with them and encourage them in their relationship with God.

You may find that it's way simpler than what I've presented. When I received Jesus, I didn't understand much of what I'm sharing with you in this chapter. All I knew was that I needed Jesus. Praise God that the Bible says, "Everyone who calls on the name of the Lord will be saved" (Romans 10:13 NIV). The thief dying on the cross next to Jesus didn't know much either, but he called on the Lord and He was saved (Luke 23:39–43).

There are many different ways to share the message. Some people use gospel tracts, or an evangecube[34], or even skits. but the bottom line is to preach the gospel! The methods change, but the message stays the same.

Common Questions

"WHAT IF THEY SAY NO?"

When you're preaching the gospel, some people may not accept the message. At the end of the day, it's their choice. You do your part and share the message. It's good to remember that Jesus is the Savior, not you. We're the messengers. Jesus said, "No one can come to Me unless the Father who sent Me draws him" (John 6:44). Pray that the Lord moves on their hearts and draws them to Jesus.

The Bible talks about the word of God being a seed and people's hearts the soil. Ask God to soften their hearts so that the seed of God's word would fall on good soil (see Matthew 13). If they receive a miracle, it's even better because they have raw evidence of the reality of Jesus.

"WHAT IF THEY WANT TO ARGUE?"

Don't get sidetracked from the message of the gospel. Keep the main thing the main thing. I've found that many times arguments are distractions. If they don't want Jesus, that's up to them, but arguing generally is a waste of time.

Be kind and give them an opportunity to receive Jesus. If they say yes, praise God! If they say no, give them another chance but don't pester them. Move on kindly when it's time.

"WHAT ABOUT HEAVEN AND HELL?"

Part of my testimony is that a Baptist preacher—thank God for the Baptists—came into Taco Bell, where I was working at the time, and preached to me. He preached the rapture and told me that if I didn't have Jesus, I'd go to hell. It's not popular preaching, but it's true and it worked. A week and a half later I got in a car accident and could have died and it was a catalyst for my coming to know Jesus. I'm glad someone gave me the raw truth.

The truth is, one thing every human being has in common is, one day, we will all die. Not to sound morbid, but unless Jesus comes back, our transition to the afterlife will be death. There is only one of two places we'll go: heaven or hell. Heaven is the dwelling place of God and hell was made for the devil and his angels. Heaven is full of life, light, and God's glory where there is no pain or sorrow. Hell is full of darkness, "[weeping] and gnashing of teeth," and torment (Luke 13:28 NIV). Jesus said that in hell the worm doesn't die, and the fire doesn't go out (see Mark 9:48).

Jesus was clear that hell was not made for people (see Matthew 25:41), however, some people will end up there. Second Thessalonians 1:9 says that those who don't know God and refuse to obey the gospel of our Lord Jesus Christ "will be punished with eternal destruction, forever separated from the Lord and from His glorious power" (NLT). To reject Jesus is to reject eternal life.

God doesn't want people to go to hell, He wants them to go to heaven. However, people have a free will to choose. God has done everything He can to get people to heaven.

> For God so loved the world that He gave His only begotten Son, that whoever believes in Him *should not perish* but have everlasting life.
>
> John 3:16

Jesus came to save us from a life without God.

> For God did not appoint us to wrath but to receive salvation through our Lord Jesus Christ. He died for us so that, whether we are awake or asleep, we may live together with Him.
>
> 1 Thessalonians 5:9–10 NIV

The reality of hell should do a couple of things to us: give us a fresh appreciation for the mercy of God and give us an urgency to share the gospel.

> **"Our goal isn't to tell people that they're going to hell, our goal is to tell people how to get to heaven.**

Our job is not to scare people into heaven. Salvation isn't a "get out of hell" card or "fire insurance." But we also can't ignore the reality of hell. Firefighters don't go into burning buildings and tell everyone they are going to burn, they go in to get people out! Yes, there is a burning building, but even more importantly, there is a way out. That's our ministry, to tell people there's a way out, and His name is Jesus!

It's completely valid to preach about heaven and hell when preaching the gospel. People don't know what day will be their last. Our goal isn't to tell people that they're going to hell, our goal is to tell people how to get to heaven.

"WHAT ABOUT FOLLOW UP?"

Jesus said to go into the world and make disciples, not converts (see Matthew 28:19). He also said "that repentance and remission of sins should be preached in His name to all nations" (see Luke 24:47).

Disciples are followers of Jesus, not just people who have prayed a prayer and haven't changed. Repentance is turning from sin and turning to God. It's a change in thinking that leads to a change in life.

Preach repentance and commitment to Christ.

As I mentioned earlier, once people have prayed to receive Christ, give them tools to grow in their relationship with Christ. Get their contact and follow up with them. Pray for them. Send them Scriptures. Ask them how their walk with Christ is going.

Discipleship is teaching others what Christ has taught you.

A Heart for Souls

Everyone was created by Jesus and their reason for existence is only found in Him. He's made the way for all people to come to Him and fulfill their purpose.

> The Lord is not slow in keeping His promise, as some understand slowness. Instead, He is patient with you, not wanting anyone to perish, but everyone to come to repentance.
> 2 Peter 3:9 NIV

God "wants all people to be saved and to come to a knowledge of the truth" (1 Timothy 2:4 NIV). God wants all people to be saved and He wants to use you to reach them. Ask God to give you His heart for souls. Salvation is the ultimate gift, and the power of God is meant to draw people to Jesus.

The harvest is now! The day of salvation is now!

Activation

PRAYER ACTIVATION

Put your hands out and pray, asking God to give you a heart for souls.

You can pray something like this:

> Lord Jesus, thank You for the price You paid at the cross. It wasn't only for me, but for the entire world; for my family, for my neighbors, and for all the people I come across. I ask that You give me Your heart for people. Fill me with Your love for souls. Give me boldness to share the gospel. Use me to lead people to Christ. Show me who I can share the gospel with. Give me Your words. Thank You, Lord. In Jesus' name, amen.

Take a few minutes and wait in His Presence. Let Him fill You with His heart and His love for souls. Meditate on the gospel message.

PREACH THE GOSPEL

- Take a moment and ask the Lord to highlight someone to you that you can share the gospel with this week.
- Be bold and share the gospel with them!
- Partner the message with a demonstration of God's power (i.e., prophetic word, word of knowledge, healing, etc.)
- Give the person an opportunity to accept Christ!

Chapter 9

The Return of the Ark

> It is time to bring back the Ark of our God, for we neglected it during the reign of Saul.
>
> David, 1 Chronicles 13:3 NLT

One thing that David did points to what God wants to do today: David returned the Presence and power of God to the people of God. Check out what God said in Amos 9:11,

> "On that day I will raise up the tabernacle of David, which has fallen down, and repair its damages; I will raise up its ruins, and rebuild it as in the days of old."

The tabernacle of David was a tent that David pitched for the Ark of the Covenant where perpetual praise went up before God and God's Presence hovered over the nation. For many years, the Ark of the Covenant was neglected and the nation suffered because of it. So, one of the first things David did when he took over as king of Israel was to bring the Ark back. He brought the Presence of God back to the center of the people of God.

Much can be said on this topic. However, I want to focus in on one thing Amos prophesied. God said He will "raise up the tabernacle of David... and rebuild it *as in the days of old.*" Well, when we look back to the days of old, we see the people of God void of the glory of God in their midst. David rose up and essentially said "We need more than what we've settled for! We need more than what we've been living in!" And he brought the Ark back.

Across the body of Christ, we need some Davids to rise up and do the same! We need more than what we've settled for. We need more than TED Talks and coffee, and music that entertains more than it brings encounter. We need more than dry, stale, crusty religion. We need the Presence and power of God in our midst! We need the Word of God to be preached and prophesied. We need an actual encounter with the living God! We need more than a visitation—we need a habitation of God's glory. People should come to our churches and gatherings and say they've met with God. That's what Paul said would happen to a church moving in power (1 Corinthians 14:25).

But, like Amos said in his day, the tent has fallen down in our day. There are places in the body of Christ that don't prioritize the Presence of God. They "[have] a form of godliness but [deny] its power" (2 Timothy 3:5 NIV). To deny means to refuse what is offered. This is like when Jesus was knocking on the door of the Laodicean church wanting to come in. They were having church without Jesus. In other words, they had program without Presence. Everyone thought they were doing great until Jesus came and prophesied to them about their true condition (Revelation 3:17–20). Lord have mercy!

It's an Amos 9–11 emergency. God wants power back in His Church. There's an urgency in the heart of God to restore His power to His people. He said He is rebuilding the Tabernacle of David. There's much more to this message, but to the point of this book, one of the ways this message manifests is the power of God flowing through His people.

This book is meant to equip you to walk in that power and I trust that it has done so thus far. The goal is that the Presence and power of God would be found in the midst of His people again. It's the return of the Ark!

Before I leave you with some practical tips, let's look a little closer at what David did.

Discipleship Happens Through an Atmosphere

People get trained by an atmosphere without even realizing it. Whatever environment you put yourself in consistently will determine what you think is normal. A powerless environment produces powerless disciples. A power-filled environment produces powerful disciples.

In the farming world, the quality of the soil determines the health of the crop. If the soil lacks nutrients, the fruit lacks vitamins. The right soil maximizes the plant's potential. The wrong soil limits the plant's ability to give you what it was meant to give you. It all comes down to soil, or we could say *environment*.

The environment contributes to the outcome. The question then becomes, what environment are you living in?

David bringing back the Ark was so significant because he was reversing the corrupt spiritual climate that had been looming over Israel. The Ark had been captured many years before because Israel lost a battle to the Philistines. The compromised priests had died in battle and upon hearing the news, one of their wives, who was pregnant, went into labor. She gave birth to a son and named him "Ichabod" for "the glory [had] departed from Israel," her main concern being the captured Ark (1 Samuel 4:19–22 NIV).

> **Whatever environment you put yourself in consistently will determine what you think is normal.**

Ichabod means "no glory." It described the spiritual condition of the nation. They were the people of God without the glory of God. They were the people of God without the Presence of God. They had all the religion but none of the glory. The problem with that is that discipleship happens in an atmosphere. When there's no glory, people are relegated to be discipled by logic and reasoning, not glory and power. Unfortunately, this could describe some church environments today. It's not just that miracles aren't happening there, it's the low-level environment that people are being mentored by.

Being discipled by Ichabod means being discipled by powerlessness. It limits what God wants to do through people's lives. Imagine being raised in an environment void of God's power. How do you think that would impact the way you think about God and life?

If you live in a powerless environment, then you'll walk away with a powerless Christianity. If you've never seen God move in healing, heard God speak, or experienced His Presence, the miraculous seems so far away. But just like the deer thirsts for the streams of water, there's a company of believers that aren't satisfied with less than what God has for them. They've got a thirst that can only be quenched by the Rivers of the Spirit of God. That was David and it should be our attitude today.

David said, "It is time to bring back the Ark of our God, for we neglected it during the reign of Saul" (1 Chronicles 13:3 NLT). He brought the Ark back! He brought the glory back! He restored the Presence of God to the people of God. The glory is the right soil or environment that maximizes our potential.

When the power of God is demonstrated, what we define as normal gets elevated. Now, imagine being raised in the revivals of old, like the Welsh Revival, Azusa Street Revival, or the San Diego Revival led by Aimee Semple McPherson I spoke about in the introduction to this book. How do you think that would impact your definition of normal?

I remember being at the Asbury revival in February 2023 for a few short days. I didn't realize what I received until I got back and started ministering. At my home church, I got to preach, and the Lord interrupted me fourteen minutes into the sermon and said, "Do an altar call for repentance." No music, no lead-in, just come. It wasn't a call to repent for sins, it was to repent for being bored with Jesus.

People came out of their seats to the front and knelt at the altar, weeping and worship followed. The power of God filled the room. I restrained myself from ministering as I usually would in the gifts because it was too holy, and I didn't want to bring any attention to myself. Jesus was the main attraction, and His glory filled the room. People lingered and just sat in His Presence. That was exactly what God was doing in Asbury and it got on me and came through me to the local church.

That's how your normal gets elevated by an atmosphere. You get in environments of glory, and you get changed.

> But we all, with unveiled face, beholding as in a mirror the glory of the Lord, are being transformed into the same image from glory to glory, just as by the Spirit of the Lord.
>
> 2 Corinthians 3:18

Today, my normal keeps getting elevated because I keep getting in the glory.

> **" We need power-filled environments so we can make some powerful disciples!**

God wants to bring His people out of Ichabod into the Kabod, which is the Hebrew word for glory. He wants to bring His glory back to the midst of His church. Discipleship happens by an atmosphere and God wants that atmosphere to be His glory. God wants to elevate your normal! The power of God isn't a side issue. The power of God is meant to be normal in every believer's life. We need power-filled environments so we can make some powerful disciples!

Tips from the Field

As this book comes to a close, I want to share some last thoughts that will help you as you step into a life of power. A life of power is a life of faith. It all works by faith. Check out these Scriptures:

> "Most assuredly, I say to you, he who *believes* in Me, the works that I do he will do also; and greater works than these he will do, because I go to My Father."
>
> John 14:12

"And these signs will follow those who *believe*: In My name they will cast out demons; they will speak with new tongues."

Mark 16:17

"Do not be afraid; only *believe*."

Mark 5:36

"According to your *faith* let it be to you."

Matthew 9:29

Let us prophesy in proportion to our *faith*.

Romans 12:6

Faith is the lifestyle of the believer. Paul said in Romans 1:17, "The righteous will live by faith," and in 2 Corinthians 5:7, "For we walk by faith, not by sight." It's not by figuring it all out, or "feeling it," it's by believing God. Faith is shown in actions.

Here are some tips from the field on walking in faith:

TAKE RISKS

John Wimber said, "Faith is spelled R–I–S–K."[35] If you haven't figured this out by now, doing all those activations at the end of the chapters in this book require risk taking. It requires stepping out on a limb with what you believe God is telling you. The risk is worth the reward!

No matter what happens, you are working your faith muscle, and someone is bound to experience the love and power of God through your faith. I know of people who had wrong words of knowledge but their conversations still led to people receiving Christ! Of course, we want to get accurate words, but the goal is that people would experience Jesus.

Be bold. Take a risk. Believe God.

KEEP AT IT

Faith is relentless. Faith is persistent.

Here's an interesting story from the Gospels. A Gentile woman comes to Jesus asking for a miracle for her daughter. Jesus denies her saying He came first for Israel. He said, "It is not right to take the children's bread and toss it to the dogs." Yikes! Jesus was not mincing His words.

This woman is completely unphased by what Jesus said and responds, "Yes, Lord, yet even the little dogs eat the crumbs which fall from their masters' table" (Matthew 15:27). And Jesus called that faith! Great faith! Her daughter was healed at that very moment.

This woman's faith was relentless. She didn't get her answer on the first try but that didn't stop her from keeping at it. Maybe you prayed for someone to get healed once and it didn't happen. Do it again! Maybe you gave a prophetic word that didn't make sense to the person you gave it to. Do it again! Maybe you tried to cast the devil out of someone, and nothing seemed to move. Do it again!

Jesus looked at a persistent woman believing for a miracle and called that faith. Keep at it!

RESIST THE RESISTANCE

When David brought the Ark back, it was a joyful praise celebration. The musicians were playing, the people were shouting, and David was dancing. The Bible said David danced "with all his might" (2 Samuel 6:14).

But there was one person who wasn't happy about this.

> Now as the ark of the Lord came into the City of David, Michal, Saul's daughter, looked through a window and saw King David leaping and whirling before the Lord; and she despised him in her heart.
>
> 2 Samuel 6:16

When David came home to bless his household, Michal criticized him to his face. Imagine the joyful celebration of God's glory being returned to His people and you got the "stink-faced" one in the corner. There's always one. Instead of backing down, David celebrated even more. He said, "I will become even more undignified than this" (2 Samuel 6:22 NIV).

Here's the truth: Not everyone is happy when revival comes. Go for it anyway! Resist the urge to be liked by everyone. Do not be led by the fear of man. Do what God says! Bill Johnson said, "If you don't live by the praises of men you won't die by their criticisms."[36]

There's another group that really doesn't like the move of God either: the Pharisees. I would like to say they were just around back in Jesus' day, but they're still around today. They're the hyper-religious folks who know everything but do nothing. They're stuck in rigid religion and really need love. When it comes to moving in power, they have every reason why what you're doing is wrong. They love to argue theology and point out the "heretics."

Now, yes, I'm being sarcastic. But in general, the overly religious kind have a hard time with the message of this book. They've been discipled by reason and logic instead of glory and power, so the things of the Spirit don't always compute.

Remember when Nicodemus, a Pharisee, came to Jesus and Jesus told him he must be born again? Nicodemus's reply was, "'How can someone be born when they are old?' Nicodemus asked. 'Surely they cannot enter a second time into their mother's womb to be born!'" (John 3:4 NIV). He went straight to limited human reasoning.

> **We need more than the limited logic of man; we need the power of God.**

This is the tragedy of being discipled by Ichabod. You come to approach spiritual things with the limited logic of man. This is why Paul said he preached, not with eloquent words of man's wisdom, but with a "demonstration" of the power of God (1 Corinthians 2:4). We need more than the limited logic of man; we need the power of God.

When Jesus was talking with the Sadducees, another religious group in Jesus' day, He said, "You are in error because you do not know the Scriptures or the power of God" (Matthew 22:29 NIV). They wanted to argue theology with Jesus and He told them that they were off because they didn't know the Scripture *or* the power. Notice He didn't say the Scriptures, period. He said the Scriptures *and* the power of God. We need both Scriptures and God's power to see and understand rightly.

The Pharisees attended one of Jesus' house meetings and the Bible says, "The power of the Lord was present to heal them" (Luke 5:17). If you follow the story, what's wild is, *none* of the Pharisees got healed. God wanted to move in their lives, yet none of them received healing. Their theology kept them from accessing the glory that was right in front of them.

Praise God the anointing in that room didn't go to waste because four men heard Jesus was there and brought their paralyzed friend to get healed. "When they could not find a way to do this because of the crowd, they went up on the roof and lowered him on his mat through the tiles into the middle of the crowd, right in front of Jesus" (Luke 5:19 NIV). Jesus spoke to him and healed the man. This paralyzed guy hijacked the healing meant for the Pharisees because his friends had faith and the Pharisees only had religion.

The kingdom of God was at hand, within reach. But they were not reaching for Jesus. All they had was criticism for Him. When you're discipled by Ichabod, you don't know what to do when the Kabod shows up.

Just like Michal, the Pharisees only had criticism for the move of God. It's the same today. You'll encounter people who criticize the joyful celebration of God's glory coming back to the church. You'll encounter those who despise the move of God. You'll encounter individuals who just want to argue theology. The religious spirit fights against the move of God.

Resist the resistance! Stand firm on truth. God is moving in power today.

DENY YOURSELF

> Then Jesus said to his disciples, "Whoever wants to be my disciple must deny themselves and take up their cross and follow me. For whoever wants to save their life will lose it, but whoever loses their life for me will find it."
>
> Matthew 16:24–25 NIV

There are going to be times when you don't *feel* like following Jesus. Specifically, for this book, there are going to be times when you don't *feel* like ministering. There are going to be times when you don't feel like praying, sharing the gospel, or showing the love of God. Do it anyway.

When I was doing campus ministry at a local university, I would have many times where I didn't feel ready, qualified, or anointed. But I would go and minister regardless, and God would move in power. There have been times in other ministry settings where I felt the resistance of spiritual warfare. But I didn't let that stop me from ministering. Many times, negative feelings and spiritual battles try hinder you from doing the works of Christ, but you must not let them stop you.

Jesus said a vital characteristic of following Him is that you must *deny yourself*. Life can be challenging, and Jesus knows our tendency to be self-centered. His answer to our self-centeredness is to die to ourselves. Jesus said if we lose our life for Him, then we would find it. Life is no longer about you, but it's about Jesus and sharing Him with the world.

Join with Paul and say,

> I have been crucified with Christ and I no longer live, but Christ lives in me. The life I now live in the body, I live by faith in the Son of God, who loved me and gave himself for me.
>
> Galatians 2:20 NIV

WALK IN LOVE

We cannot overemphasize love. Paul said, "And now these three remain: faith, hope and love. But the greatest of these is love" (1 Corinthians 13:13 NIV). In the middle of teaching on spiritual gifts, Paul inserts an entire chapter on love and its importance.

People aren't projects. Treat them with dignity. Treat them with kindness. Including the Pharisees. They honestly sometimes just need a hug, and don't we all? Power is a vehicle to get the love of God to people.

> The only thing that counts is faith expressing itself through love.
>
> Galatians 5:6 NIV

STAY CONNECTED TO JESUS AND COMMUNITY

> "I am the vine; you are the branches. If you remain in Me and I in you, you will bear much fruit; apart from Me you can do nothing."
>
> Jesus, John 15:5 NIV

Stay prayerful. Stay in the Word. Stay in community.

One of the best places to practice the things in this book is at church. Granted, you need to follow the guidelines and authority in place at your church. But most of the things I've taught in this book came because I was plugged into a local church. When Jesus sent the disciples out to minister the kingdom in power, He sent them out, not alone, but two by two (see Mark 6:7–13, Luke 10:1).

A good community has leaders you're accountable to, peers you can run with, and people you can pour into. I encourage you to find a community that does the following things:

- Worships passionately
- Prays fervently
- Loves the Word of God
- Lives pure and holy lives
- Walks in power
- Joyfully follows Jesus
- A community that lives in the glory

As you step out in faith to walk in power, ask some trusted friends to be praying for you. Ask them to pray for you to have boldness, protection, and favor. The apostle Paul consistently asked for prayer as he endeavored to make Jesus known. We would do well to follow his example.

It's Time to Do Something

A while back, our family was taking a walk in our neighborhood during October. Since it was "Halloween season," many were decorating their houses accordingly. Except it felt like it was much darker than when I was a kid. Without going into detail, there were some dark decorations out there! It looked like hell threw up on these front lawns.

> **The anointing comes to *do something*.**

I thought, *If they can put hell on display in their front yard, I can put heaven on display in mine!* I was literally thinking of how I could get the four living creatures with eyes all around, a throne, and a lamb looking as if it had been slain to display on my front lawn (see Revelation 4–5). I was going to take "on earth as it is in heaven" quite literally (Matthew 6:10)!

Well, the budget didn't quite make it for all those decorations, but we did try to host heaven on our front yard. Instead of complaining about how dark Halloween is, we just did an outreach in our driveway! Someone once said, "It's better to light a candle than to curse the darkness." We set up a table, made a cheap cardboard sign that said, "Free Spiritual Blessings," gave out candy, and ministered the gospel. Some of our friends came over and ministered with us.

We led two girls to Jesus, a couple of people got healed, and a bunch of people received prayer! We took one of the best opportunities and did something with it. Think about it. This is the one day out of the year when people are coming to your house expecting to receive something. Give them Jesus!

The anointing comes to *do something*. God anoints you to do something.

> "The Spirit of the Lord is upon Me, because He has anointed Me *to preach* the gospel to the poor; He has sent Me *to heal* the brokenhearted, *to proclaim* liberty to the captives and recovery of sight to the blind, *to set at liberty* those who are oppressed; *to proclaim* the acceptable year of the Lord."
>
> Luke 4:18–19
>
> How God anointed Jesus of Nazareth with the Holy Spirit and with power, who went about doing good and healing all who were oppressed by the devil, for God was with Him.
>
> Acts 10:38

We do not get the anointing so we can just sit in it. We get the anointing so we can do something. You wouldn't make it this far in the book if you weren't the kind of person who wanted to do something.

Have you ever been at a friend's house and the group wants to play a new board game? Then someone tries to teach everyone how to play and after a few minutes you kind of get it—but not really—and then you all end up saying, "Let's just play and we'll get it as we go." That's how it can be with ministry.

You can keep on reading more and more books, go to more seminars, and online courses, but it's only when you start doing something that you'll start seeing results! And you'll learn as you go.

It's time to put your faith into action and see God move and grow you!

New Normal

I'm sure, by now, you have plenty of testimonies of God working already. Don't stop! This is your new normal. This is the return of the Ark!

The goal of this book has been to make power the norm in your life. The goal of the activations is to help you put the Word into action. Events are a catalyst for a lifestyle. This book is a launching pad for a new normal.

It's time to joyfully bring in the Presence of God to your church, to your city, to your family, to your neighborhood. Welcome the Spirit of God to move in power and point people to Jesus!

Activation

GLORY COMMUNITY

As described in this book, having a godly community is vital to growing as a follower of Jesus who walks in power.

Gather a group of friends to seek the Lord together. Take time to worship and pray, and specifically pray for each other. Ask God what gifts He wants to employ during your time together and go for it!

As a bonus step: Take it to the streets! Pray and ask the Lord where He would have your group go and share the power and love of Jesus.

RE-ACTIVATE THE ACTIVATIONS

Go back and do one of the activations at the end of one of the chapters.

Endnotes

1 Aimee Semple McPherson, This Is That (International Church of the Foursquare Gospel,1923), 248–304.

2 McPherson, This Is That, 279-292

3 "Leaning Tower of Pisa," Brittanica, Last updated June 13, 2024, https://www.britannica.com/topic/Leaning-Tower-of-Pisa.

4 "Burj Khalifa Fact Sheet," Burj Khalifa, Accessed June 13, 2024, https://www.burjkhalifa.ae/img/FACT-SHEET.pdf.

5 Simmons, Brian. "The Love of God." Sermon at SoCal School of Ministry, September 21, 2022.

6 "Tackling Foundations: Essential Techniques for Stable Building Structures", The Constructor, Accessed July 2, 2024, https://theconstructor.org/structural-engg/foundation-design/tackling-foundations-essential-techniques-for-stable-building-structures/571452/#google_vignette.

7 Bill Johnson, When Heaven Invades Earth (Shippensburg, PA: Treasure House/Destiny Image, 2003), 119.

8 "Witness," Dictionary.com, Accessed June 13, 2024, https://www.dictionary.com/browse/witness. I first learned that a "witness" produces evidence in the context of supernatural ministry through Morris Cerullo. Morris Cerullo, The Power of Pentecost (San Diego, CA: Morris Cerullo World Evangelism, 2014), 35–36.

9 McPherson, This Is That, 260–261

10 Bill Johnson, When Heaven Invades Earth, 122–123. I have gleaned so much about the purpose of miracles from Bill Johnson.

11 "G1411 - dynamis - Strong's Greek Lexicon (kjv)." Blue Letter Bible. Accessed 14 Jun, 2024. https://www.blueletterbible.org/lexicon/g1411/kjv/tr/0-1/.

12 Darren Wilson, director. Holy Ghost. Featuring Bill Johnson and others. Wanderlust Productions, 2014. 1 hour 52 minutes. https://www.amazon.com/gp/video/detail/

B00R16KRD6/ref=atv_dp_share_cu_r/.

13   "Ode to the Spirit," Words and music by Andrew Hopkins. © Breaker Ministries.

14   Blaise Pascal, Pensees, trans. A. J. Krailsheimer (London: Penguin, 1993), 45. I am using a paraphrased statement derived from what Pascal has said.

15   Saint Augustine, Confessions (Oxford: Oxford University Press, 1992) 3n1.

16   "G3875 - paraklētos - Strong's Greek Lexicon (kjv)." Blue Letter Bible. Accessed 14 June 2024. https://www.blueletterbible.org/lexicon/g3875/kjv/tr/0-1/.

17   Jack Hayford, executive editor, Word Wealth section, Dick Mills, "New Spirit-Filled Life Bible (Nashville: Thomas Nelson, 2002), 1470

18   Hayford, New Spirit-Filled Life Bible, 1470

19   "H3519 - kāḇôḏ - Strong's Hebrew Lexicon (kjv)." Blue Letter Bible. Accessed 14 Jun, 2024. https://www.blueletterbible.org/lexicon/h3519/kjv/wlc/0-1/

20   "H3513 - kāḇaḏ - Strong's Hebrew Lexicon (kjv)." Blue Letter Bible. Accessed 14 Jun, 2024. https://www.blueletterbible.org/lexicon/h3513/kjv/wlc/0-1/.

21   "G3618 - oikodomeō – Strong's Greek Lexicon (kjv)." Blue Letter Bible. Accessed 14 Jun, 2024. https://www.blueletterbible.org/lexicon/g3618/kjv/tr/0-1/.

22   Mahesh Chavda, The Hidden Power of Speaking In Tongues, (Shippensburg: Destiny Image, 2003), 86

23   "G2909 - kreittōn – Strong's Greek Lexicon (kjv)." Blue Letter Bible. Accessed 14 June 2024. https://www.blueletterbible.org/lexicon/g2909/kjv/tr/0-1/.

24   "H5012 - nāḇā' – Strong's Hebrew Lexicon (kjv)." Blue Letter Bible. Accessed 15 June 2024. https://www.blueletterbible.org/lexicon/h5012/kjv/wlc/0-1/

25   Sam Storms, The Beginner's Guide to Spiritual Gifts, (Bloomington: Bethany House Publishers, 2012), 145

26   T.L. Osborn, Healing The Sick, (Tulsa: Harrison House, 1992), 223.

27   "The Supernatural Power of a Transformed Mind – Bill Johnson Ministries," n.d., Accessed June 15, 2024, https://bjm.org/core-values/the-supernatural-power-of-a-transformed-mind/.

28   One example of the many videos is this one: Todd White, "Todd White – Healing on the Streets of Jerusalem (Israel – Part 9) YouTube video, 7:40, February 8, 2018, Accessed June 15, 2024, https://youtu.be/V_1EPmA9bLw?si=26s85bcfKPv0JE_h/.

29   "The Spurgeon Library | the Story of God's Mighty Acts." n.d. The Spurgeon Center. Accessed June 15, 2024. https://www.spurgeon.org/resource-library/sermons/the-story-of-gods-mighty-acts/#flipbook/.

30 "H4886 - māšaḥ - Strong's Hebrew Lexicon (kjv)." Blue Letter Bible. Accessed 15 Jun, 2024. https://www.blueletterbible.org/lexicon/h4886/kjv/wlc/0-1/.

31 Bill Johnson and Randy Clark, The Essential Guide to Healing, (Bloomington: Chosen Books, 2011), 220–240

32 "Renounce", Dictionary.com, Accessed June 15, 2024, https://www.dictionary.com/browse/renounce

33 Kenneth E. Hagin, The Believer's Authority (Legacy Edition) (Tulsa: Faith Library Publications, 2004), 11

34 "The EvangeCube by E3 Resources is a seven-picture cube that simply and clearly unfolds the gospel of Jesus Christ. Highly portable and usable in any language, the EvangeCube is a preferred tool for mission trips and church outreach events." "E3 Resources | Creators of Evangecube." n.d. E3 Resources. Accessed June 17, 2024. https://e3resources.org/.

35 "Quotes from John Wimber." 2016. Vineyard USA. March 25, 2016. Accessed June 17, 2024, https://vineyardusa.org/quotes-from-john-wimber/

36 Bill Johnson, "Facebook" May 14, 2011, Accessed June 17, 2024, https://www.facebook.com/BillJohnsonMinistries/posts/if-you-dont-live-by-the-praises-of-men-you-wont-die-by-their-criticisms/10150181003393387/.

About the Author

Andrew Hopkins is a revivalist, prophetic worship leader, author, and revelatory preacher and teacher. Through his itinerate ministry, Breaker Ministries, Andrew travels and ministers at various churches and events. He has a passion for the gospel of Jesus, equipping the saints, and seeing God move in supernatural ways. He has been leading worship since 2002 at his local church and churches, at various events/conferences, and in the nations. He is an anointed songwriter, has released multiple worship albums, and excels in equipping worship ministries.

Andrew also works as a teaching pastor and worship director at REV Church in north San Diego, CA. Andrew has earned a Bachelor of Arts in Christian Studies in Worship from Vision International University. He and his beautiful wife Rochelle have two boys, Hunter & Everett.

Find out more or invite Andrew to minister at
www.breakerministries.com

Join our email list and receive a FREE 7-day devotional on praise. Sign up at www.breakerministries.com

Follow Andrew on social media:

- Instagram: @andrewwhopkins
- Facebook: facebook.com/AndrewHopkinsBreaker
- YouTube: @breakerministries

Music

Listen to Andrew's music at **www.breakerministries.com**, and all online music platforms: Spotify, Apple Music, etc.

More Books by Andrew Hopkins

Find Andrew's books at **www.breakerministries.com** and on Amazon.

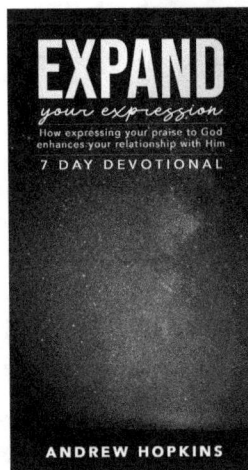

Worship ministry training through teaching articles, training videos, and online courses & coaching.

Find out more at
www.breakerworshipschool.com

www.ingramcontent.com/pod-product-compliance
Lightning Source LLC
Chambersburg PA
CBHW072157070526
44585CB00015B/1187